English - Spanish

EDITORIAL
Polaris

INDEX

USE OF THIS GUIDE

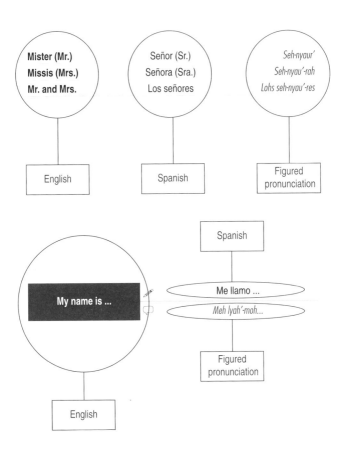

FIGURED PRONUNCIATION

Spanish words are pronounced exactly as they are written, except for a few exceptions (the silent *h* and the two symbols *b/v* for the same sound).

So, we can say that the pronunciation is not at all difficult; nevertheless, we offer you a figured pronunciation based on comparisons with English sounds for a practical use, if lacking the scientific exactness of the International Phonetic Alphabet.

All we want is to encourage you to speak Spanish from the start!

VOWELS	Like in ...	Represented by ...
a	f*a*ther	*ah*
e	b*e*d, th*e*y	*eh*
i	t*i*p, f*ee*	*e, ee*
o	A*u*gust	*au, oh*
u	f*oo*d	*oo*

CONSONANTS WITH SPECIAL DIFFICULTY

	Like in ...	Represented by ...
b, v	bom*b*	*b, v*
c	*th*in (before e, i)	*th*
	*c*at (before a, o, u)	*c*
	*h*ost (before e, i)	*h*
g	*h*ost (before e, i)	*h*
	*g*o (before a, o, u)	*gh*
h	always silent	
j	*h*ost (stronger)	*h*
ll	mil*li*on	*ly*
ñ	o*ni*on	*ny*

q	king	k
r	road (final or interior)	r
	strongly trilled	r-r
	(when doubled or initial)	
y	yes, day (when final)	y
z	thin	th

In **diphthongs** you pronounce every single vowel: causa (*kah'-oo-sah*), **Eu**ropa (*Eh-oo-rau'-pah*).

STRESS

Words ending in a *vowel*, in *n* or in *s*, are stressed on the next of the last syllable: mesa, orden, niños.

Words ending in *any other consonant* are stressed on the last syllable: señor, Madrid, general.

If a word does not conform with these two rules, an acute accent (') is written over the vowel of the stressed syllable: café, capitán, inglés, Málaga.

In this Guide it is represented by (').

A SHORT GUIDE TO SPANISH GRAMMAR

1. ARTICLES

THE DEFINITE ARTICLE

Before a masculine noun,   *sing.* **el** *libro* (the book).
                            pl. **los** *libros* (the books).
Before a feminine noun*,   *sing.* **la** *casa* (the house).
                            pl. **las** *casas* (the houses).

When the article *el* comes after the prepositions *de* (or or from) or *a* (to), a contraction takes place: *de el = del, a el = al.*
Before adjectives with abstract meaning the neuter form **lo** is used: **lo** *bello* (the beautiful, what is beautiful).

THE INDEFINITE ARTICLE

Before a masculine noun,   *sing.* **un** *hombre* (a man).
                            pl. **unos** *hombres* (some men).
Before a feminine noun*,   *sing.* **una** *mesa* (a table).
                            pl. **unas** *mesas* (some tables).

*The forms *el, un* are used before a feminine noun beginning with the stressed sound *a* or *ha*: *el agua fresca* (the fresh water), *un hacha afilada* (a sharp axe).

2. NOUNS

Gender.

Nouns belong either to the masculine or the feminine gender. The natural gender is maintained in nouns like: *el padre* (father), *la madre* (mother); *el rey* (king), *la reina* (queen); *el toro* (bull), *la vaca* (cow).

Nouns ending in *-o* are generally masculine: *el vino* (wine).
Exceptions: *la mano* (hand), *la foto* (photo), *la moto* (scooter).

Nouns ending in *-a, -ción, -sión, -dad, -tad* are feminine: *la ventana* (window), *la habitación* (room), *la ciudad* (town).
Exceptions: *el día* (day), *el tranvía* (tram) and nouns of Greek origin ending in *-ma*: *el clima* (climate), *el problema* (problem).

There are no special rules for nouns ending otherwise: *el mes* (month), *la flor* (flower), *el autobús* (bus), *la miel* (honey).

Number.

The plural of nouns is formed by adding *-s* to nouns ending in unstressed vowel or stressed *-é*: *puerta* (door), *puertas* (doors); *café* (coffee house), *cafés* (coffee houses).

Nouns terminating in consonant add *-es*: *tren* (train), *trenes* (trains); *color* (colour), *colores* (colours). The letter *z* is replaced by *c* before *-es*: *luz* (light), *luces* (lights).
Masculine plural forms may refer to a mixed set of both masculine and feminine: *los padres* (parents), *los hermanos* (brothers and sisters), *los chicos* (boys and girls).

3. ADJECTIVES

Adjectives agree with their nouns in gender and number. Adjectives and nouns are inflected alike; e. g. he comido *una naranja* muy *buena* (I have eaten a very good orange); *estos plátanos* son muy *buenos* (these bananas are very good).
If adjectives end in -o, they have 4 forms: *malo, mala, malos, malas* (bad).
Adjectives not ending in -o have only 2 forms: *verde, verdes* (green); *fácil, fáciles* (easy).
Exception: The adjectives denoting a nationality, with 4 forms:
inglés, inglesa, ingleses, inglesas.
Adjectives generally follow their noun: *corbata azul* (blue tie).
Some adjectives standing before a masculine singular noun lose their final vowel or syllable:
bueno: un *buen* vino (a good wine).
malo: *mal* tiempo (bad weather).
primero: el *primer* piso (the first floor).
tercero: el *tercer* hombre (the third man).
grande: un *gran* palacio (a big palace).
Santo: San Pedro (Saint Peter).

Comparison of Adjectives. The comparative of superiority is formed with **más ... que* (more or -er than); that of inferiority, with *menos ... que* (less ... than); that of equality, with *tan ... como* (as/so ... as).
The relative superlative is rendered by prefixing the definite article to the comparative of superiority: *el más largo* (the longest), *la más guapa* (the more beautiful).
The absolute superlative is formed by prefixing the adverb *muy* to the adjective or by adding to it the termination *-ísimo: muy bueno* or *buenísimo* (very good).
*Some adjectives have special forms: *mejor* (better), *peor* (worse), *mayor* (greater, larger, older), *menor* (smaller, younger).

4. PRONOUNS

A pronoun replaces a noun in a sentence. Certain pronouns as e. g. the posessive, demonstrative, interrogative and indefinite pronouns have the same form and meaning as the corresponding adjectives, which are followed by a noun.

PERSONAL PRONOUNS

yo (I)	*me* (me)	**mí* (me)
tú (you)	*te* (you)	**ti* (you)
él (he)	*le* (him), *lo* (him, it)	
ella (she)	*le* (her), *la* (her, it)	
*usted (you)	*le*	
nosotros (-as) (we)	*nos* (us)	
vosotros (-as) (you)	*os* (you)	
ellos (-as) (they)	*les, los, las* (them)	
*ustedes (you)	*les*	

*Usted (Vd.) and *ustedes (Vds.)* are used when you want to be more formal (similar to using Mr... or Ms... instead of first names) and take the verb in the third person.

The personal subject pronouns do not normally appear with the verb, because its forms indicate the subject by themselves; nevertheless, *Vd.* and *Vds.* appear more frequently than other pronouns: *Usted no tiene razón* (You're not right).

The object pronouns precede the verb, except when it is an infinitive, a gerund or an affirmative imperative; e. g. *Te espero* (I'm waiting for you), but *Démelo* (Give it to me).

*Mí and *ti* are used when a preposition precedes.

REFLEXIVE PRONOUNS differ from the objective forms only in the third person (sing. and plur.): *Se lava* (he/she washes himself/herself), but *Me lavo* (I wash myself).

POSSESSIVE ADJECTIVES AND PRONOUNS

mi, mis (my)	*mío, -a, -os, -as* (mine)
tu, tus (your)	*tuyo, -a, -os, -as* (yours)
su, sus (his, her, its)	*suyo, -a, -os, -as* (his, hers, its)
nuestro, -a, -os, -as (both: our and ours)	
vuestro, -a, -os, -as (both: your and yours)	
su, sus (their)	*suyo, -a, -os, -as* (their)

In case of ambiguity instead of *su, suyo* a paraphrase is used:
su carta: la carta de él (de ella, de usted, de ellos, de ellas, de ustedes).

DEMONSTRATIVE ADJECTIVES AND PRONOUNS

Spanish divides space into 3 separate planes: *aquí* (the area which is relatively close to the speaker), *ahí* (an intermediate area which is near the hearer) and *allí* (the area distant for both, the speaker and the hearer). Consequently, there are 3 kinds of demonstrative adjectives and pronouns:

este, esta, *esto, estos, estas (this, these)
ese, esa, *eso, esos, esas (that, those -near you-)
aquel, aquella, *aquello, aquellos, aquellos (that, those-there-)

**Esto, eso , aquello* are "neuter" pronouns and are used to refer to something when we do not know what it is or we do not wish to mention its name.

RELATIVE AND INTERROGATIVE ADJECTIVES AND PRONOUNS

> *quien, quienes* (who)
> *¿quién/quiénes?* (who?)
> *que* (who, which, that)
> *¿qué?* (what?)
> *el/la cual, los/las cuales* (which)
> *¿cuál/cuáles?* (which one-s?)

All interrogative adjectives and pronouns bear a written accent mark to distinguish them from the corresponding relative.

An inverted question mark is put at the beginning of the interrogative sentence in written Spanish.

INDEFINITE ADJECTIVES AND PRONOUNS

> *cada, cada uno* (each/every, everyone)
> *otro, -a, -os, -as* (other, another)
> *todo, -a, -os, -as* (all, whole)
> *todo el mundo* (everybody)
> *varios, -as* (several)
> *mucho, -a, -os, -as* (much, many)
> *demasiado, -a, -os, -as* (too, too much, too many)
> **alguno, -a, -os, -as* (some, any)
> **ninguno, -a* (no, none)
> *alguien* (somebody, anybody)
> *algo* (something, anything)
> *nadie* (nobody)
> *nada* (nothing)
> *poco, -a, -os, -as* (little, few)
> **cualquiera* (any, whoever, whichever)

*When preceding a masculine noun, the short forms *algún, ningún* are used. Also, *cualquier* before a noun (masc. or femin.).

5. ADVERBS

Many adverbs are formed from adjectives by adding the suffix -*mente* to the feminine form: *solamente* (only), *normalmente* (normally).

In compound tenses, the adverb cannot take its place between the auxiliary and the participle, as in English: *Ya* ha venido/Ha venido *ya* (He has already come).

According to the meaning, they are the following kinds of adverbs in Spanish:

of time

hoy (today)	*ya* (already)
ayer (yesterday)	*todavía* (still, yet)
anteayer (the day before yesterday)	*temprano* (early)
mañana (tomorrow)	*tarde* (late)
pasado mañana (the day after tomorrow)	*ahora* (now)
antes (before)	*pronto* (soon)
después (after, afterwards)	*luego* (later)
otra vez (again)	*entonces* (then)

of frequency

siempre (always)	*dos veces* (twice)
nunca (never)	*alguna vez* (ever)
algunas veces (sometimes)	*normalmente* (usually)
a menudo (often)	*muchas veces* (many times)
una vez (once)	

of degree

casi (nearly, almost)	*apenas* (hardly)
muy (very)	*totalmente* (totally)
bastante (quite, fairly)	

of manner

bien (well)	*despacio* (slowly)
mal (badly)	*rápidamente* (quickly)

and most of the adverbs ending in -*mente*.

of place

aquí (here)
ahí (there)
allí (over there)
cerca (near)
lejos (far, away)
dentro (in, inside)
en todas partes (everywhere)

delante (in front of)
detrás (behind)
enfrente (opposite)
arriba (up, upstairs)
abajo (down, downstairs)
alrededor (around)
fuera (out, outside)

of probability

quizá (maybe, perhaps)
posiblemente (possibly)

probablemente (probably)
a lo mejor (probably)

of affirmation/negation

sí (yes)
no (no)
en absoluto (not at all)

verdaderamente (indeed)
por supuesto (of course)

relative

cuando (when)
por que, por lo que (why)

donde (where)

interrogative

¿cuándo? (when?)
¿dónde? (where?)

¿por qué? (why?)

6. PREPOSITIONS

a (to, at)

acerca de (about, concerning)

además de (besides, in addition)

al lado de (beside)

con (with)

contra (against)

de (of, from)

desde (from, since)

durante (during)

en (in, on, into)

entre (between, among)

hacia (towards)

hasta (till, until)

junto a (close, next to)

para (for, in order to)

sobre (on, over, about)

respecto a (in relation to)

según (according to)

sin (without)

7. CONJUNCTIONS

y (and)

o (or)

ni (nor, neither)

también (also, too, as well)

tampoco (not... either)

pero (but)

sin embargo (nevertheless)

para que (so that)

como (as, since)

cuando (when)

mientras (while, whereas)

porque (because)

si (if, whether)

ni siquiera (not even)

aunque (although)

entonces (then)

8. VERBS

According to the termination of the infinitive, Spanish verbs fall into three conjugations: 1. verbs ended in -ar, as *hablar* (to speak); 2. verbs ending in -er, as *comer* (to eat); 3. verbs terminating in
-ir, as *vivir* (to live).
All verbal terminations are added to the radical which you get by omitting the ending -ar, -er, -ir respectively.

COMPOUND TENSES are formed by means of the corresponding tense of the auxiliary verb *haber* (to have) (see List of Irregular Verbs) and the past participle of the verb that is conjugated: *He trabajado* (I have worked).

The NEGATIVE CONJUGATION is rendered by placing the adverb *no* before the verb: *No hablo* (I do not speak).

The INTERROGATIVE CONJUGATION is obtained by placing the subject after the verb: *¿Está Elena?* Is Helen in?

REGULAR VERBS

Infinitive	Gerund	Past Participle
habl/ar	habl/ando	habl/ado
com/er	com/iendo	com/ido
viv/ir	viv/iendo	viv/ido

INDICATIVE	Present	**(hablar).** habl/o, -as, -a, -amos, -áis, -an. **(comer).** com/o, -es, -e, -emos, -éis, -en. **(vivir).** viv/o, -es, -e, -imos, -ís, -en.
	Simple past	habl/é, -aste, -ó, -amos, -asteis, -aron. com/í, -iste, -ió, -imos, -isteis, -ieron. viv/í, -iste, -ió, -imos, -isteis, -ieron.
	Imperfect past	habl/aba, -abas, -aba, -ábamos, -abais, -aban. com/ía, -ías, -ía, -íamos, -íais, -ían. viv/ía, -ías, -ía, -íamos, -íais, -ían.
	Future	hablar/é, comer/é, -ás, -á, -emos, -éis, -án. escribir/é,
	Conditional	hablar/ía, comer/ía, -ías, -ía, -íamos, -íais, -ían. vivir/ía,
IMPERATIVE		habl/a, -e, -emos, -ad, -en. com/e, -a, -amos, -ed, -an. viv/e, -a, -amos, -id, -an.
SUBJUNCTIVE	Present	habl/e, -es, -e, -emos, -éis, -en. com/a, -as, -a, -amos, -áis, -an. viv/a, -as, -a, -amos, -áis, -an.
	Past	habl/ara, -aras, -ara, -áramos, -arais, -aran. habl/ase, -ases, -ase, -ásemos, -aseis, -asen. com/iera, com/iese, -ieras, -iera, -iéramos, -ierais, -ieran. viv/iera, viv/iese, -ieses, -iese, -iésemos, -ieseis, -iesen.

IRREGULAR VERBS

In this short summary of the most usual verbs, irregular forms are indicated in italics and it does not appear regular tenses.

SER (to be; also auxiliary for the passive voice)

Pres.	*soy, eres, es, somos, sois, son*
Past. Simp.	*fui, fuiste, fue, fuimos, fuisteis, fueron*
Imperfect	*era, eras, era, éramos, erais, eran*

HABER (to have; used only as an auxiliary verb)

Pres.	*he, has, ha, hemos, habéis, han*
Future	*habré, habrás, habrá, habremos, habréis, habrán*

ESTAR (to be, to be in, to stand, to be present)

Pres.	estoy, estás, está, estamos, estáis, *están*
Past. Simp.	*estuve, estuviste, estuvo, estuvimos, estuvisteis, estuvieron*

TENER (to have, to have got, to possess)

Pres.	*tengo,* tienes, tiene, tenemos, tenéis, *tienen*
Past. Simp.	*tuve, tuviste, tuvo, tuvimos, tuvisteis, tuvieron*
Future	*tendré, tendrás, tendrá, tendremos, tendréis, tendrán*

HACER (to do, to make)

Pres.	*hago,* haces, hace, hacemos, hacéis, hacen
Past. Simp.	*hice, hiciste, hizo, hicimos, hicisteis, hicieron*
Future	*haré, harás, hará, haremos, haréis, harán*

DECIR (to say, to tell)

Pres.	*digo,* dices, dice, decimos, decís, *dicen*
Past. Simp.	*dije, dijiste, dijo, dijimos, dijisteis, dijeron*
Future	*diré, dirás, dirá, diremos, diréis, dirán*

IR (to go)

Pres.	*voy, vas, va, vamos, vais, van*
Past. Simp.	*fui, fuiste, fue, fuimos, fuisteis, fueron*
Imperfect	*iba, ibas, iba, íbamos, ibais, iban*

VENIR (to come)

Pres.	*vengo, vienes, viene, venimos, venís, vienen*
Past. Simp.	*vine, viniste, vino, vinimos, vinisteis, vinieron*
Future	*vendré, vendrás, vendrá, vendremos, vendréis, vendrán*

SALIR (to go out, to leave, to depart)

Pres.	*salgo, sales, sale, salimos, salís, salen*
Future	*saldré, saldrás, saldrá, saldremos, saldréis, saldrán*

SABER (to know)

Pres.	*sé, sabes, sabe, sabemos, sabéis, saben*
Past. Simp.	*supe, supiste, supo, supimos, supisteis, supieron*
Future	*sabré, sabrás, sabrá, sabremos, sabréis, sabrán*

QUERER (to want, to wish, to love, to like)

Pres.	*quiero, quieres, quiere, queremos, queréis, quieren*
Past. Simp.	*quise, quisiste, quiso, quisimos, quisisteis, quisieron*
Future	*querré, querrás, querrá, querremos, querréis, querrán*

NUMBERS

1.	Uno.	*Oo'-noh*
2.	Dos.	*Daus*
3.	Tres.	*Tres*
4.	Cuatro.	*Coo-ah'-troh*
5.	Cinco.	*Theen'-coh*
6.	Seis.	*Seh'-ees*
7.	Siete.	*Se-eh'-teh*
8.	Ocho.	*Au'-choh*
9.	Nueve.	*Noo-eh'-veh*
10.	Diez.	*De-eth'*
11.	Once.	*Aun'-theh*
12.	Doce.	*Dau'-theh*
13.	Trece.	*Treh'-theh*
14.	Catorce.	*Cah-taur'-theh*
15.	Quince.	*Keen'-theh*
16.	Dieciséis.	*De-eh-the-seh'-ees*
17.	Diecisiete.	*De-eh-the-se-eh'-teh*
18.	Dieciocho.	*De-eh-the-au'-choh*
19.	Diecinueve.	*De-eh-the-noo-eh'-veh*
20.	Veinte.	*Veh'-in-teh*
21.	Veintiuno.	*Veh-in-te-oo'-noh*
22.	Veintidós.	*Veh-in-te-daus'*
23.	Veintitrés.	*Veh-in-te-tres'*
24.	Veinticuatro.	*Veh-in-te-coo-ah'-troh*
30.	Treinta.	*Treh'-in-tah*
40.	Cuarenta.	*Coo-ah-rehn'-tah*
50.	Cincuenta.	*Thin-coo-ehn'-tah*
60.	Sesenta.	*Seh-sehn'-tah*
70.	Setenta.	*Seh-tehn'-tah*
80.	Ochenta.	*Au-chehn'-tah*
90.	Noventa.	*Nau-vehn'-tah*
100.	Cien.	*The-ehn'*

200.	Doscientos.	*Daus-the-ehn'-tohs*
300.	Trescientos.	*Trehs-the-ehn'-tohs*
400.	Cuatrocientos.	*Coo-ah-troh-the-ehn'-tohs*
500.	Quinientos.	*Kee-ne-ehn'-tohs*
600.	Seiscientos.	*Seh-ees-the-ehn'-tohs*
700.	Setecientos.	*Seh-teh-the-ehn'-tohs*
800.	Ochocientos.	*Au-choh-the-ehn'-tohs*
900.	Novecientos.	*Noh-ve-the-ehn'-tohs*
1.000.	Mil.	*Meel*
2.000.	Dos mil.	*Daus' meel*
5.000.	Cinco mil.	*Theen'-coh meel*
10.000.	Diez mil.	*De-eth' meel*
100.000.	Cien mil.	*The-ehn' meel*
1.000.000.	Un millón.	*Oon mil-lyaun'*

1st	Primero.	*Pre-meh'-roh*
2nd	Segundo.	*Seh-goon'-doh*
3rd	Tercero.	*Ter-theh'-roh*
4th	Cuarto.	*Coo-ar'-toh*
5th	Quinto.	*Keen'-toh*
6th	Sexto.	*Sex'-toh*
7th	Séptimo.	*Sep'-te-moh*
8th	Octavo.	*Auk-tah'-voh*
9th	Noveno.	*Nau-veh'-noh*
10th	Décimo.	*Deh'-the-moh*

1/2.	Medio.	*Meh'-de-oh*
1/3.	Un tercio.	*Oon ter'-the-oh*
1/4.	Un cuarto.	*Oon coo-ar'-toh*
1/5.	Un quinto.	*Oon keen'-toh*
1/10	Un décimo.	*Oon deh'-the-moh*

WEIGHTS AND MEASURES

Length

1 cm. (centímetro)	= 0,3937 inch	= 0,0328 foot
1 m. (metro)	= 3,2808 feet	= 1,0936 yards
1 km. (kilómetro)		= 0,6213 mile

Weight

1 kg. (kilogramo)	= 2,2050 pounds

Capacity

1 l. (litro)	= 0,212 gallon	= 1,756 pints

Temperature
0° C = 32° F

To convert F. degrees to C. deduct 32 and multiply by 5/9.

EVERYDAY LIFE

GREETINGS

Good morning	Buenos días	*Boo-eh'-nohs dee'-ahs*
Good afternoon	Buenas tardes	*Boo-eh'-nahs tar'-dehs*
Good evening	Buenas tardes/ noches	*Boo-eh'-nahs tar'-dehs/nau'-chehs*
Good night	Buenas noches	*Boo-eh'-nahs nau'-chehs*
Hello	Hola	*Au'-lah*
Goodbye	Adiós	*Ah-de-aus'*
See you later	Hasta luego	*As'-tah loo-eh'-goh*
See you tomorrow	Hasta mañana	*As'-tah mah-nyah'-nah*
See you soon	Hasta pronto	*As'-tah praun'-toh*
How do you do?	¿Cómo está Vd.?	*Cau'-moh es-tah' oos-ted'?*
How are you?	¿Cómo estás?	*Cau'-moh es-tahs'?*
How are you?	¿Qué hay?/¿Qué tal?	*Keh' ah'-y?/Keh' tahl?*
How are you getting on?	¿Cómo te/le va?	*Cau'-moh teh/leh vah?*
(Very) well	(Muy) bien	*(Moo'-y) be-en'*
All right	Muy bien	*Moo'-y be-en'*
Thank you	Gracias	*Grah'-the-ahs*

How is your family?	✏️ ¿Cómo está su (tu) familia?
	💬 *Cau'-moh es-tah' soo (too) fah-mee'-le-ah?*

I am glad	✏️ Me alegro
	💬 *Meh ah-leh'-groh*

| Nice to see you again | Me alegro de volver a verle |
| | *Meh ah-leh'-groh deh vaul-ver' ah ver'-leh* |

| It has been a long time! | ¡Cuánto tiempo sin verle! |
| | *Coo-ahn'-toh te-ehm'-poh sin ver'-leh!* |

| How do you feel today? (to a sick person) | ¿Cómo se encuentra hoy? |
| | *Cau'-moh seh en-coo-ehn'-trah au'-y?* |

| Give my regards to everybody | Recuerdos a todos |
| | *Reh-coo-er'-dohs ah tau'-dohs* |

| Give my love to the children | Besos a los niños |
| | *Beh'-sohs ah lohs nee'-nyohs* |

INTRODUCTIONS

Mister (Mr.)	Señor (Sr.)	*Seh-nyaur'*
Missis (Mrs.)	Señora (Sra.)	*Seh-nyau'-rah*
Mr. and Mrs.	Los señores	*Lohs seh-nyau'-res*
Sir	Señor	*Seh-nyaur'*
Madam	Señora	*Seh-nyau'-rah*

| My name is ... | Me llamo ... |
| | *Meh lyah'-moh...* |

| How do you do? | Mucho gusto |
| | *Moo'-choh goos'-toh* |

| Pleased to meet you | Encantado/a |
| | *En-can-tah'-doh/-dah* |

| What is your name? | ¿Cómo te llamas/ se llama Vd.? |
| | *Cau'-moh teh lyah'-mas?/ Cau'-moh seh lya'-mah oos-ted'?* |

| This is Mr. ... This is Ms. ... | Este es el Sr. ... Esta es la Sra. ... |
| | *Es'-teh es el seh-nyaur'... Es'-tah es lah seh-nyau'-rah ...* |

| Let me introduce you... | Le presento a... |
| | *Leh preh-sehn'-toh ah...* |

| I would like to introduce you to... | Quiero presentarle a ... |
| | *Ke-eh'-roh preh-sen-tar'-leh ah...* |

| Have you met Mr....? | ¿Conoce ya al Sr....? |
| | *Cau-nau'-theh yah ahl seh-nyaur'...?* |

| Are you Mr. (Mrs.) ...? | ¿Es usted el señor (la señora) ...? |
| | *Es oos-ted' el seh-nyaur' (lah seh-nyau'-rah) ...?* |

| Yes, I am he (she) | Sí, soy yo |
| | *See', sau'-y yoh* |

PERSONAL PARTICULARS

Name	Nombre	*Naum'-breh*
Surname	Apellido	*Ah-peh-lyee'-doh*
Age	Edad	*Eh-dad'*
Marital status	Estado civil	*Es-tah'-doh the-veel'*
Single	Soltero	*Saul-teh'-roh*
Married	Casado	*Cah-sah'-doh*
Divorced	Divorciado	*De-vaur-the-ah'-doh*
Widow(er)	Viudo(a)	*Ve-oo'-doh(ah)*
Profession	Profesión	*Prau-feh-se-aun'*
Address	Dirección	*De-rec-the-aun'*
Passport	Pasaporte	*Pah-sah-paur'-teh*
Identity card number	D.N.I.	*Deh-ehne-ee*
Date of birth	Fecha de nacimiento	*Feh'-chah deh nah-the-me-en'-toh*
Place of birth	Lugar de nacimiento	*Loo-gar deh nah-the-me-en'-toh*

What is your name?
¿Cómo se llama Vd.?/
¿Cuál es su nombre?

Cau'-moh seh lyah'-mah oos-ted'?/
Coo-ahl' es soo naum'-breh?

What is your address?
¿Cuál es su dirección?

Coo-ahl' es soo de-rec-the-aun'?

| Where do you live? | ¿Dónde vive? |
| | *Daun'-deh vee'-veh?* |

| What is your phone number? | ¿Cuál es su número de teléfono? |
| | *Coo-ahl' es su noo'-meh'-roh deh teh-leh'-fau-noh?* |

| Where are you from?/ What is your nacionality? | ¿De dónde es Vd.?/ ¿Cuál es su nacionalidad? |
| | *Deh daun'-deh es oos-ted'?/ Coo-ahl' es soo nah-the-au-nah-le-dad'?* |

| How old are you? | ¿Cuántos años tiene? |
| | *Coo-ahn'-tohs ah'-nyohs te-eh'-neh?* |

| I was born in ... | Nací en ... |
| | *Nah-thee' ehn ...* |

SHORT QUESTIONS AND ANSWERS

Who is it?	¿Quién es?	*Ke-ehn' es?*
What is that?	¿Qué es eso?	*Keh' es eh'-soh?*
Where is it?	¿Dónde está?	*Daun'-deh es-tah'?*
Why?	¿Por qué?	*Paur keh'?*
Which one?	¿Cuál?	*Coo-ahl'?*
How much/many?	¿Cuánto/-a/-os/-as?	*Coo-ahn'-toh/ah/ohs/ahs?*
Are you sure?	¿Seguro?	*Seh-goo'-roh?*
Really?	¿De verdad?	*Deh ver-dad'?*

O.K.?	¿Vale?	*Vah'-leh?*
Yes	Sí	*See'*
All right (O.K.)	De acuerdo (Vale)	*Deh ah-coo-er'-doh (vah'-leh)*
That's right	Es verdad	*Es ver-dad'*
Of course	Por supuesto	*Paur soo-poo-ehs'-toh*
You are right	Tiene Vd. razón	*Te-eh'-neh oos-ted' rah-thaun'*
I see	Ya entiendo	*Yah en-te-ehn'-doh*
No	No	*Noh*
Not at all	En absoluto	*En ab-sau-loo'-toh*
Never	Nunca	*Noon'-cah*
Nothing	Nada	*Nah'-dah*
It is wrong	No es así	*Noh es ah-see'*
I do not think so	No creo	*Noh creh'-oh*

POLITE PHRASES

Thank you very much	Muchas gracias	*Moo'-chas grah'-the-ahs*
You are welcome (don't mention it)	De nada	*Deh nah'-dah*
Please	Por favor	*Paur fah-vaur'*
Would you please...?	Haga el favor	*Ah'-gah el fah-vaur'*
It is a pleasure	Con mucho gusto	*Caun moo'-choh goos'-toh*
Excuse me	Disculpe	*Dis-cool'-peh*
Pardon	Perdón	*Per-daun'*
Sorry	Perdón / Lo siento	*Per-daun'/Loh se-ehn'-toh*
Welcome!	¡Bienvenido!	*Be-en-veh-nee'-doh!*

English	Spanish	Pronunciation
Cheers!	¡Salud!	*Sah-lood'!*
Congratulations	¡Felicidades!	*Feh-le-the-dah'-des!*
Congratulations	¡Enhorabuena!	*En-au'-rah-boo-eh-nah!*
Good luck	¡Suerte!	*Soo-er'-teh!*

It does not matter	No importa	*Noh im-paur'-tah*
Here you are	Aquí tiene	*Ah-kee' te-eh'-neh*
May I help you?	¿Le puedo ayudar?	*Leh poo-eh'-doh ah-yoo-dar'?*
You are very kind	Es usted muy amable	*Es oos-ted' moo'-e ah-mah'-bleh*
Don't bother	No se moleste	*Noh seh mau-les'-teh*
Sorry to trouble you	Siento molestarle	*Se-ehn'-toh mau-les-tar'-leh*
Thank you very much	Se lo agradezco mucho	*Seh loh ah-grah-deth'-coh moo'-choh*
Don't worry!	¡No se preocupe!	*Noh seh preh-au-coo'-peh!*
Don't mention it!	¡No hay de qué!	*Noh ah'-y deh keh'!*

| What can I do for you? | ¿En qué puedo servirle? |
| | *En keh' poo-eh'-doh ser-veer'-leh?* |

| Would you like something to drink? | ¿Desea tomar algo? |
| | *Deh-seh'-ah tau-mar' ahl'-goh?* |

| Would you like a cigarette? | ¿Quiere un cigarrillo? |
| | *Ke-eh'-reh oon the-gar-ree'-lyoh?* |

| Do you want something? | ¿Desea algo? |
| | *Deh-seh'-ah al'-goh?* |

| I would like ... | Quería (quisiera) ... |
| | *Keh-ree'-ah (ke-se-eh'-rah)...* |

LEARNING THE LANGUAGE

| Do you speak English? | ¿Habla Vd. inglés? |
| | *Ah'-blah oos-ted' in-gles'?* |

| I do not speak Spanish | No hablo español |
| | *Noh ah'-bloh es-pah-nyau'* |

| A little bit | Un poco |
| | *Oon pau'-coh* |

| Not one word | Ni una palabra |
| | *Nee oo'-nah pah-lah'-brah* |

| Do you understand me? | ¿Me comprende? |
| | *Meh caum-prehn'-deh?* |

I do not understand	🖊	No comprendo/entiendo
	💬	*Noh caum-prehn'-doh / en-te-ehn'-doh*
Pardon?	🖊	¿Cómo?/¿Perdón?
	💬	*Cau'-moh?/Per-daun'?*
Speak slowly, please	🖊	Hable Vd. más despacio, por favor
	💬	*Ah'-bleh oos-ted' mas des-pah'-the-oh, paur fah-vaur'*
How do you write it?	🖊	¿Cómo se escribe?
	💬	*Cau'-moh seh es-cree'-beh?*
Can you spell it, please?	🖊	Deletréelo, por favor
	💬	*Deh-leh-treh'-eh-loh, paur fah-vaur'*
How do you pronounce it?	🖊	¿Cómo se pronuncia?
	💬	*Cau'-moh seh prau-noon'-the-ah?*
What do you mean?	🖊	¿Qué quiere usted decir?
	💬	*Keh' ke-eh'-reh oos-ted' deh-theer'?*
How do you say ... in Spanish?	🖊	¿Cómo se dice ... en español?
	💬	*Cau'-moh seh dee'-theh ... en es-pah-nyaul'?*
What did you say?	🖊	¿Cómo dice?
	💬	*Cau'-moh dee'-theh?*
Could you repeat, please?	🖊	Repita, por favor
	💬	*Reh-pee'-tah, paur fah-vaur'*
What are you saying?	🖊	¿Qué dice Vd.?
	💬	*Keh' dee'-theh oos-ted'?*

ORDERS

Hurry up!	¡Deprisa!	*Deh-pree'-sah!*
Slowly!	¡Despacio!	*Des-pah'-the-oh!*
Quickly!	¡Rápido!	*Rah'-pe-doh!*
Come in!	¡Entre! ¡Adelante!	*Ehn'-treh! Ah-deh-lahn'-teh!*
Come here!	¡Venga!	*Vehn'-gah!*
Come on!	¡Venga!	*Vehn'-gah!*
Listen!	¡Oiga!	*Au'-e-gah!*
Give me!	¡Déme!	*Deh'-meh!*
Be careful!	¡Cuidado!	*Coo-e-dah'-doh!*
Sit down!	¡Siéntese!	*Se-ehn'-teh-seh!*
Help!	¡Socorro!	*Sau-caur'-roh!*
Silence	Silencio	*Se-lehn'-the-oh*
Let's go!	¡Vamos!	*Vah'-mos!*
Go ahead!	¡Adelante!	*Ah-deh-lahn'-teh!*
Shut up!	¡Cállese!	*Cah'-lyeh-seh!*

PUBLIC NOTICES

Caution	Cuidado	*Coo-e-dah'-doh*
Danger	Peligro	*Peh-lee'-groh*
Beware of...	Atención al...	*Ah-ten-the-aun' ahl ...*
Closed	Cerrado	*Ther-rah'-doh*
Open	Abierto	*Ah-be-er'-toh*
Out of order	Averiado	*Ah-veh-re-ah'-doh*
Entrance	Entrada	*En-trah'-dah*

Exit	Salida	*Sah-lee'-dah*
Lift	Ascensor	*As-then-saur'*
Vacant	Libre	*Lee'-breh*
Engaged	Ocupado	*Au-coo-pah'-doh*
Private	Privado	*Pre-vah'-doh*
Pull	Tirar	*Te-rar'*
Push	Empujar	*Em-poo-har'*
(Bus) stop	Parada	*Pah-rah'-dah*
Toilets	Servicios	*Ser-vee'-the-ohs*
Ladies	Señoras	*Seh-nyau'-rahs*
Men	Caballeros	*Cah-bah-lyeh'-rohs*
Exchange	Cambio	*Cahm'-be-oh*
For sale	Se vende	*Seh vehn'-deh*
For rent (hire)	Se alquila	*Seh ahl-kee'-lah*
Parking	Aparcamiento	*Ah-par-cah-me-ehn'-toh*
Self-service	Autoservicio	*Ah-oo-tau-ser-vee'-the-oh*
Reception	Recepción	*Reh-thep-the-aun'*

Keep out
Prohibido el paso
Prau-e-bee'-doh el pah'-soh

No smoking
Prohibido fumar
Prau-e-bee'-doh foo-mar'

No admittance
Se prohíbe la entrada
Seh prau-ee'-beh lah en-trah'-dah

Wet paint
Recién pintado
Reh-the-en' pin-tah'-doh

TIME AND WEATHER

Time	Tiempo	*Te-ehm'-poh*
Hour	Hora	*Au'-rah*
Watch	Reloj	*Reh-lau'*
Minute	Minuto	*Me-noo'-toh*
Second	Segundo	*Seh-goon'-doh*
Half an hour	Media hora	*Meh-de-ah au'-rah*
Morning	Mañana	*Mah-nyah'-nah*
Noon	Mediodía	*Meh-de-au-dee'-ah*
Afternoon	Tarde	*Tar'-deh*
Evening	Tarde	*Tar'-deh*
Night	Noche	*Nau'-cheh*
Midnight	Medianoche	*Meh-de-ah-nau'-cheh*

What time is it?	¿Qué hora es?
	Keh' au'-rah es?

It is seven o'clock	Son las siete
	Saun lahs se-eh'-teh

Ten past seven	Las siete y diez
	Lahs se-eh'-teh ee de-eth'

A quarter past seven	Las siete y cuarto
	Lahs se-eh'-teh ee coo-ar'-toh

Half past seven	Las siete y media
	Lahs se-eh'-teh ee meh-de-ah

A quarter to eight	Las ocho menos cuarto
	Lahs au'-choh meh'-nohs meh'-de-coo-ar'-toh

Can you tell me the time, please?	¿Puede decirme la hora, por favor?
	Poo-eh'-deh deh-theer'-meh lah au'-rah, paur fah-vaur'?

What time does the museum open?	¿A qué hora abre el museo?
	Ah keh' au'-rah ah'-breh el moo-seh'-oh?

It is too early (late)	Es demasiado temprano (tarde)
	Es deh-mah-se-ah'-doh tem-prah'-noh (tar'-deh)

Weather	Tiempo	*Te-ehm'-poh*
Temperature	Temperatura	*Tem-peh-rah-too'-rah*
Climate	Clima	*Klee'-mah*

It is sunny	Hace sol
	Ah'-theh saul

It is cold	Hace frío
	Ah'-theh free'-oh

It is hot	Hace calor
	Ah'-theh cah-laur'

It is windy	Hace viento
	Ah'-theh ve-ehn'-toh

It is cloudy	Está nublado
	Es-tah' noo-blah'-doh

I am cold	Tengo frío
	Tehn'-goh free'-oh

| It is raining | ✏️ | Está lloviendo |
| | 💬 | *Es-tah' lyau-ve-ehn'-doh* |

| It is going to rain | ✏️ | Va a llover |
| | 💬 | *Vah ah lyau-ver'* |

| It is still raining | ✏️ | Sigue lloviendo |
| | 💬 | *See'-gheh lyoh-ve-ehn'-doh* |

| It has stopped raining | ✏️ | Ha dejado de llover |
| | 💬 | *Ah deh-hah'-doh deh yau-ver'* |

| It is snowing | ✏️ | Está nevando |
| | 💬 | *Es-tah' neh-vahn'-doh* |

| It is freezing | ✏️ | Está helando |
| | 💬 | *Es-tah' eh-lahn'-doh* |

| What is the weather like? | ✏️ | ¿Qué tiempo hace? |
| | 💬 | *Keh' te-ehm'-poh ah'-theh?* |

| The weather is bad | ✏️ | Hace mal tiempo |
| | 💬 | *Ah'-theh mal te-ehm'-poh* |

| It is a fine day | ✏️ | Hace un tiempo magnífico |
| | 💬 | *Ah'-theh oon te-ehm'-poh mag-nee'-fe-coh* |

| It is minus six (degrees) | ✏️ | Estamos a seis grados bajo cero |
| | 💬 | *Es-tah'-mos ah seh'-es grah'-dohs bah'-hoh theh'-roh* |

Day	Día	*Dee'-ah*
Week	Semana	*Seh-mah'-nah*
Month	Mes	*Mehs*

Fortnight	Quincena	*Keen-theh'-nah*
Year	Año	*Ah'-nyoh*
Century	Siglo	*See'-gloh*
Today	Hoy	*Au'-y*
Yesterday	Ayer	*Ah-yer'*
Tomorrow	Mañana	*Mah-nyah'-nah*
Tonight	Esta noche	*Es'-tah nau'-cheh*
Bank Holiday	Día festivo	*Dee'-ah fes-tee'-voh*
Date	Fecha	*Feh'-chah*

DAYS OF THE WEEK

Monday	Lunes	*Loo'-nehs*
Tuesday	Martes	*Mar'-tehs*
Wednesday	Miércoles	*Me-er'-cau-lehs*
Thursday	Jueves	*Hoo-eh'-vehs*
Friday	Viernes	*Ve-er'-nehs*
Saturday	Sábado	*Sah'-bah-doh*
Sunday	Domingo	*Dau-meen'-goh*

MONTHS OF THE YEAR

January	Enero	*Eh-neh'-roh*
February	Febrero	*Feh-breh'-roh*
March	Marzo	*Mar'-thoh*
April	Abril	*Ah-breel'*
May	Mayo	*Mah'-yoh*
June	Junio	*Hoo'-ne-oh*
July	Julio	*Hoo'-le-oh*
August	Agosto	*Ah-gaus'-toh*

September	Septiembre	*Sep-te-ehm'-breh*
October	Octubre	*Auc-too'-breh*
November	Noviembre	*Nau-ve-ehm'-breh*
December	Diciembre	*De-the-ehm'-breh*

SEASONS

Winter	Invierno	*In-ve-er'-noh*
Spring	Primavera	*Pree-mah-veh'-rah*
Summer	Verano	*Veh-rah'-noh*
Autumn	Otoño	*Au-tau'-nyoh*

Last Sunday	✏️ El domingo pasado
	💬 *El dau-meen'-goh pah-sah'-doh*

Next Monday	✏️ El lunes próximo
	💬 *El loo'-nehs prauc'-se-moh*

6th November 1995	✏️ El seis de noviembre de mil novecientos noventa y cinco
	💬 *El seh'-ees deh nau-ve-ehm'-breh deh meel nau-veh-the-ehn'-tohs nau-vehn'-tah ee theen'-coh*

What is the day today?	✏️ ¿Qué día es hoy?
	💬 *Keh' dee'-ah es au'-y?*

Today is the first of April	✏️ Hoy es uno de abril
	💬 *Au'-y es oo'-noh deh ah-breel'*

Christmas	Navidad	*Nah-ve-dad'*
New Year's Day	Año Nuevo	*Ah'-nyoh Noo-eh'-voh*
Easter (Holy Week)	Semana Santa	*Seh-mah'-nah sahn'-tah*
May Day	Primero de Mayo	*Pree-meh'-roh deh mah'-yoh*

IN TOWN

Street, road	Calle	*Cah'-lyeh*
Avenue	Avenida	*Ah-veh-nee'-dah*
Promenade	Paseo	*Pah-seh'-oh*
City centre	Centro	*Thehn'-troh*
Street corner	Esquina	*Es-kee'-nah*
Suburb (district)	Barrio	*Bar'-re-oh*
Outskirts	Afueras	*Ah-foo-eh'-rahs*
Port (harbour)	Puerto	*Poo-er'-toh*
Fountain	Fuente	*Foo-ehn'-teh*
Square	Plaza	*Plah'-thah*
Bridge	Puente	*Poo-ehn'-teh*
River	Río	*Ree'-oh*
Garden	Jardín	*Har-deen'*
Park	Parque	*Par'-keh*
Subway	Paso subterráneo	*Pah'-soh soob-ter-rah'-neh-oh*
Crossroads	Cruce	*Croo'-theh*
Traffic-lights	Semáforo	*Seh-mah'-fau-roh*
Traffic policeman	Guardia de tráfico	*Goo-ar'-de-ah deh trah'-fe-coh*
Litter bin	Papelera	*Pah-peh-leh'-rah*
Pillar box	Buzón	*Boo-thaun'*
Street light	Farola	*Fah-rau'-lah*
Telephone box	Cabina	*Cah-bee'-nah*
Pavement	Acera	*Ah-theh'-rah*
Zebra crossing	Paso de cebra	*Pah'-soh deh theh'-brah*

| This way | ✏ | Por aquí |
| | 💬 | *Paur ah-kee'* |

| That way | ✏ | Por ahí |
| | 💬 | *Paur ah-ee'* |

| Straight on | ✏ | Todo recto |
| | 💬 | *Tau'-doh rehc'-toh* |

| To the left | ✏ | A la izquierda |
| | 💬 | *Ah lah ith-ke-er'-dah* |

| To the right | ✏ | A la derecha |
| | 💬 | *Ah lah deh-reh'-chah* |

| ... metres from here | ✏ | A... metros de aquí |
| | 💬 | *Ah... meh'-trohs deh ah-kee'* |

In front of	Delante de	*Deh-lahn'-teh deh*
Behind	Detrás de	*Deh-tras' deh*
Opposite	Enfrente	*En-frehn'-teh*
Further on (back)	Más adelante (atrás)	*Mas ah-deh-lahn'-teh (ah-tras')*
Further up (down)	Más arriba (abajo)	*Mas ar-ree'-bah (ah-bah'-hoh)*

| Excuse me, is ... street far from here? | ✏ | Perdón, ¿está muy lejos la calle ...? |
| | 💬 | *Per-daun', es-tah' moo'-y leh'-hohs lah cah'-lyeh ...?* |

| Can you tell me where ... is? | ✏ | ¿Puede Vd. decirme dónde está ...? |
| | 💬 | *Poo-eh'-deh oos-ted' deh-theer'-meh daun'deh es-tah'...?* |

| How do you get to...? | ✏ | ¿Cómo se va a ...? |
| | 💬 | *Cau'-moh seh vah ah ...?* |

Is it very far?	¿Está muy lejos?	*Es-tah' moo'-y leh'-hohs?*
How far away is...?	¿A qué distancia está...?	*Ah keh' dis-tahn'-the-ah es-tah'...?*
Go straight on along this street	Siga por esta misma calle	*See'-gah paur es'-tah mees'-mah cah'-lyeh*
On the other side of the road	Al otro lado de la calle	*Ahl au'-troh lah'-doh deh lah cah'-lyeh*
It is the road parallel to this one	Es la paralela a ésta	*Es lah pah-rah-leh'-lah ah es'-tah*
It is a long way, you'd better take the bus	Está muy lejos, es mejor que tome el autobús	*Es-tah' moo'-y leh'-hohs, es meh-haur' keh tau'-meh el ah-oo-tau-boos'*
Follow me, I am going in that direction too	Sígame, yo también voy en esa dirección	*See'-gah-meh, yoh tam-be-en' voh'-y en eh'-sah de-rec-the-aun'*
It is very difficult to explain	Es muy difícil de explicar	*Es moo'-y de-fee'-thihl deh ex-ple-car'*
Round the corner	Al doblar la esquina	*Ahl dau-blar' lah es-kee'-nah*

PUBLIC BUILDINGS

Town Hall	Ayuntamiento	*Ah-yoon-tah-me-ehn'-toh*
Court	Juzgado	*Hooth-gah'-doh*
County council	Diputación	*De-poo-tah-teh-aun'*
Embassy	Embajada	*Em-bah-hah'-dah*
Consulate	Consulado	*Caun-soo-lah'-doh*
Post office	Correos	*Caur-reh'-ohs*
Police station	Comisaría	*Cau-me-sah-ree'-ah*
Hospital	Hospital	*Aus-pe-tahl'*
Tourist office	Oficina de Turismo	*Au-fe-thee'-nah deh too-rees'-moh*
Station	Estación	*Es-tah-the-aun'*
Castle	Castillo	*Cas-tee'-lyoh*
Palace	Palacio	*Pah-lah'-the-oh*
Church	Iglesia	*E-gleh'-se-ah*
Cathedral	Catedral	*Cah-teh-drahl'*
Museum	Museo	*Moo-seh'-oh*
School	Escuela	*Es-coo-eh'-lah*
Institute	Instituto	*Ins-te-too'-toh*
University	Universidad	*Oo-ne-ver-se-dad'*
Public library	Biblioteca pública	*Be-ble-au-teh'-cah poo'-ble-cah*
Cemetery	Cementerio	*Theh-men-teh'-ree-oh*
Bull ring	Plaza de toros	*Plah'-thah deh deh tau'-rohs*

TRAVELLING

AT A TRAVEL AGENCY

I want to go to ... by plane

Quiero ir a ... en avión

Ke-eh'-roh eer ah ... en ah-ve-aun'

I would like to leave next week

Me gustaría salir la semana próxima

*Meh goos-tah-ree'-ah sah-leer'
lah seh-mah'-nah prauc'-se-mah*

I would like to make the trip by coach and stay at two star hotels

Quisiera hacer el viaje en autocar y alojarme en hoteles de dos estrellas

*Ke-se-eh'-rah ah-thehr' el ve-ah'-heh en
ah-oo-tau-car' ee ah-loh-har'-meh en au-teh'-les
deh daus es-treh'-lyahs*

I would like to visit the ... region

Desearía visitar la región de ...

Deh-seh-ah-ree'-ah ve-se-tar' lah reh-he-aun' deh...

What towns do you advise me to visit?

¿Qué ciudades me aconseja que visite?

*Keh' the-oo-dah'-dehs meh ah-caun-seh'-hah
keh ve-see'-teh?*

Could you prepare me an itinerary and an estimate?

¿Podría hacerme un itinerario y un presupuesto?

*Pau-dree'-ah ah-ther'-meh oon e-te-neh-rah'-re-oh
ee oon pre-soo-poo-es'-toh?*

What does that all cost?

¿Cuánto cuesta todo eso?

Coo-an'-toh coo-es'-tah tau'-doh eh'-soh?

Book me two seats on ...'s coach	✏️ Resérveme dos plazas en el autocar del...
	💬 *Reh-ser'-veh-meh daus plah'-thahs en el ah-oo-tau-car' dehl ...*

All right. I'll pick up my ticket tomorrow	✏️ De acuerdo. Mañana vendré a recoger mi billete
	💬 *Deh ah-coo-er'-doh. Mah-nyah'-nah ven-dreh' ah reh-cau-her' mee be-lyeh'-teh*

Have you got any tourist brochures?	✏️ ¿Tiene usted folletos turísticos?
	💬 *Te-eh'-neh oos-ted' fau-lyeh'-tohs too-rees'-te-cos?*

AT THE CUSTOMS

Customs	Aduana	*Ah-doo-ah'-nah*
Documentation	Documentación	*Dau-coo-men-tah-the-aun'*
Passport	Pasaporte	*Pah-sah-paur'-teh*
Luggage	Equipaje	*Eh-kee-pah'-heh*
Case (suitcase)	Maleta	*Mah-leh'-tah*
Present, gift	Regalo	*Reh-gah'-loh*
Handbag	Bolso de mano	*Baul'-soh deh mah'-noh*
Passport control	Control de pasaportes	*Caun-traul' deh pah-sah-paur'-tes*
Customs duties licence	Derechos de aduana	*Deh-reh'-chohs deh ah-doo-ah'-nah*
International driving licence	Permiso internacional de conducir	*Per-mee'-soh in-ter-nah-the-au nal' deh caun-doo-theer'*
Green card	Carta verde	*Car'-tah ver'-deh*
Entry visa	Visado de entrada	*Ve-sah'-doh deh en-trah'-dah*

Passport, please	Por favor, su pasaporte
	Paur fah-vaur', soo pah-sah-paur'-teh
Here you are	Aquí tiene
	Ah-kee' te-eh'-neh
The purpose of my journey is to ...	El objeto de mi viaje es ...
	El aub-heh'-toh deh mee ve-ah'-heh es ...
Holidays, touring, family affairs, studies	Vacaciones, turismo, asuntos familiares, estudios
	Vah-cah-the-au'-nes, too-rees'-moh, ah-soon'-tohs fah-me-le-ah'-rehs, es-too'-de-ohs
Have you got anything to declare?	¿Tiene Vd. algo que declarar?
	Te-eh'-neh oos-ted' al'-goh keh deh-clah-rar'?
I haven't got anything to declare	No tengo nada que declarar
	Noh tehn'-goh nah'-dah keh deh-clah-rar'
No, I only have personal effects	No, sólo llevo objetos de uso personal
	Noh, sau'-loh lyeh'-voh aub-heh'-tohs deh oo'-soh per-sau-nal'
I have some bottles of wine and cigarettes	Llevo unas botellas de vino y cigarrillos
	Lyeh'-voh oo'-nas bau-teh'-lyas deh vee'-noh ee the-gar-ree'-lyohs
I haven't got any foreign currency	No llevo moneda extranjera
	Noh lyeh'-voh mau-neh'-dah ex-tran-heh'-rah

Open your bags, please	Abra sus maletas, por favor
	Ah'-brah soos mah-leh'-tahs, paur fah-vaur'

What have you got in these parcels?	¿Qué lleva Vd. en esos paquetes?
	Keh' lyeh'-vah oos-ted' en eh'-sos pah-keh'-tehs?

May I close my cases?	¿Puedo cerrar mis maletas?
	Poo-eh'-doh ther-rar' mees mah-leh'-tahs?

How much duty have I to pay?	¿Cuánto tengo que pagar de derechos?
	Coo-ahn'-toh tehn'-goh keh pah-gar' deh deh-reh'-chohs?

Is everything O.K.?	¿Está todo en orden?
	Es-tah' tau'-doh en aur'-den?

Where is the exchange office?	¿Dónde está la oficina de cambio?
	Daun'-deh es-tah' lah au-fe-thee'-nah deh cahm'-be-oh?

What is the rate for the euro?	¿Cuál es la cotización del euro?
	Coo-ahl' es lah cau-te-tha-the-aun' dehl eh'-oo-roh?

Can you change me ... into euros?	¿Puede cambiarme ... en euros?
	Poo-eh'-deh cahm-be-ar'-meh ... en eh'-oo-ros?

Where are the taxis?	¿Dónde hay taxis?
	Daun'-deh ah'-y tac'-ses?

BY PLANE

Airport	Aeropuerto	*Ah-eh-rau-poo-er'-toh*
Passenger	Pasajero	*Pah-sah-heh'-roh*
Timetable	Horario	*Au-rah'-re-oh*
Check-in desk	Facturación	*Fac-too-rah-the-aun'*
Ticket	Billete	*Be-lyeh'-teh*
Airlines	Líneas aéreas	*Lee'-neh-ahs ah-eh'-reh-ahs*
Flight	Vuelo	*Voo-eh'-loh*
Arrivals	Llegadas	*Lyeh-gah'-dahs*
Departures	Salidas	*Sah-lee'-dahs*
Plane	Avión	*Ah-ve-aun'*
Pilot	Piloto	*Pe-lau'-toh*
Stewardess	Azafata	*Ah-thah-fah'-tah*
Seat	Asiento	*Ah-se-ehn'-toh*
(Non) smoker	(No) fumador	*(Noh) foo-mah-daur'*
Window	Ventanilla	*Ven-tah-nee'-lyah*
Crew	Tripulación	*Tre-poo-lah-the-aun'*
Delay	Retraso	*Reh-trah'-soh*
Excess weight	Exceso de equipaje	*Ex-theh'-soh deh eh-ke-pah'-heh*
Boarding pass	Tarjeta de embarque	*Tar-heh'-tah deh em-bar'-keh*
Departures lounge	Sala de espera	*Sah'-lah deh es-peh'-rah*
Gate	Puerta de embarque	*Poo-er'-tah deh em-bar'-keh*
Flight cancelled	Vuelo suspendido	*Voo-eh'-loh soos-pen-dee'-doh*
Life jacket	Chaleco salvavidas	*Chah-leh'-coh sal-vah-vee'-dahs*
Lost and found	Objetos perdidos	*Aub-heh'-tohs per-dee'-dohs*

The flight to ... (from...)	El vuelo con destino a ... (procedente de ...)
	El voo-eh'-loh caun des-tee'-noh ah (prau-theh-dehn'-teh deh)

How soon should we be at the airport before take-off?	¿Con qué antelación hay que estar en el aeropuerto?
	Caun keh' an-teh-lah-the-aun' ah'-y keh es-tar' en el ah-eh-roh-poo-er'-toh?

How can I get to the airport?	¿Cómo puedo ir al aeropuerto?
	Cau'-moh poo-eh'-doh eer ahl ah-eh-rau-poo-er'-toh?

What weight am I allowed?	¿Cuánto peso está permitido?
	Coo-ahn'-toh peh'-soh es-tah' per-me-tee'-doh?

What time does the plane to ... leave?	¿A qué hora sale el avión para ...?
	Ah keh' au'-rah sah'-leh el ah-ve-aun' pah'-rah ...?

Passengers for flight ... go to gate ...	Se ruega a los pasajeros del vuelo... embarquen por la puerta...
	Seh roo-eh'-gah ah lohs pah-sah-heh'-ros del voo-eh'-loh ... em-bar'-ken paur lah poo-er'-tah ...

Hurry up! We are been called over the loudspeaker	¡Deprisa! Nos están llamando por los altavoces
	Deh-pree'-sah! Naus es-tahn' lyah-mahn'-doh paur lohs al-tah-vau'-thehs

| Fasten your seat belts, please | ✏️ Por favor, abróchense los cinturones |
| | 💬 *Paur fah-vaur', ah-brau'-chen-seh lohs thin-too-rau'-nehs* |

| No smoking | ✏️ Prohibido fumar |
| | 💬 *Prau-e-bee'-doh foo-mar'* |

| We shall land in ten minutes | ✏️ Tomaremos tierra dentro de diez minutos |
| | 💬 *Toh-mah-reh'-mos te-er'-rah den'-troh deh de-eth' me-noo'-tohs* |

| Pick up your luggage at the terminus | ✏️ Recojan su equipaje en la terminal |
| | 💬 *Reh-cau'-hahn soo eh-ke-pah'-heh en lah tehr-me-nal'* |

| One of my suitcases has been lost | ✏️ Se me ha perdido una maleta |
| | 💬 *Seh meh ah per-dee'-doh oo'-nah mah-leh'-tah* |

BY TRAIN

Train	Tren	*Trehn*
Station	Estación	*Es-tah-the-aun'*
Platform	Andén	*An-dehn'*
Track	Vía	*Vee'-ah*
Carriage	Vagón	*Vah-gaun'*
Sleeper	Litera	*Le-teh'-rah*
Compartment	Compartimento	*Caum-par-te-mehn'-toh*
Passenger	Viajero	*Ve-ah-heh'-roh*
Inspector	Revisor	*Reh-ve-saur'*
Bag	Bolsa	*Baul'-sah*
Rucksack	Mochila	*Mau-chee'-lah*
Briefcase	Maletín	*Mah-leh-teen'*

Single (return) ticket	Billete de ida (de ida y vuelta)	Be-lyeh'-teh deh ee'-dah (deh ee'-dah ee v oo-el'-tah)
1st, 2nd class	Primera, segunda clase	Pree-meh'-rah, seh-goon'-dah clah'-seh
Sleeping car	Coche-cama	Cau'-cheh cah'-mah
Timetable	Cuadro de horarios	Coo-ah'-droh deh au-rah'-re-ohs
Left-luggage office	Consigna	Caun-seeg'-nah
Ticket office	Despacho de billetes	Des-pah'-choh deh be-yeh'-tehs
Inter City, short distance train, express train	Talgo, tren de cercanías, tren directo	Tahl'-goh, trehn deh ther-cah-nee'-as, trehn de-rec'-toh

Where is the railway station?

¿Dónde está la estación de trenes?

Daun'-deh es-tah' lah es-tah-the-aun' deh treh'-nes?

What is the quickest way of getting to the station?

¿Cómo puedo llegar a la estación lo antes posible?

Cau'-moh poo-eh'-doh lyeh-gar' ah lah es-tah-the-aun' loh ahn'-tes pau-see'-bleh?

Can you take me to the station? I am in a great hurry!

¡Lléveme a la estación. Tengo mucha prisa!

Lyeh'-veh-meh ah lah es-tah-the-aun'. Tehn'-goh moo'-chah pree'-sah!

At which ticket office do I get a ticket to ...?

¿En qué ventanilla despachan los billetes para ...?

En keh' ven-tah-nee'-lyah des-pah'-chan lohs be-lyeh'-tehs pah'-rah ...?

How much does a return ticket to ... cost?	¿Cuánto cuesta un billete de ida y vuelta a ...?
	Coo-ahn'-toh coo-es'-tah oon be-lyeh'-teh deh ee'-dah ee voo-el'-tah ah ...?
Is there a half price ticket for students/children/pensioners?	¿Hay descuentos para estudiantes/ niños/pensionistas?
	Ah'-y des-coo-en'-tohs pah'-rah es-too-de-ahn'-tes/ nee'-nyohs/pen-se-au-nees'-tahs?
Two tickets to ...	Dos billetes para ...
	Daus be-lyeh'-tehs pah'-rah ...
By which train?	¿Para qué tren?
	Pah'-rah keh' trehn?
Is there a train to...?	¿Hay un tren para ...?
	Ah'-y oon trehn pah'-rah...?
Is this the train for...?	¿Es éste el tren para ...?
	Es es'-teh el trehn pah'- pah'-rah ...?
What time does the train to ... leave?	¿A qué hora sale el tren para ...?
	Ah keh' au'-rah sah'-leh el trehn pah'-rah ...?
Which platform does the train to ... leave from?	¿De qué andén sale el tren para ...?
	Deh keh' an-dehn' sah'-leh el trehn pah'-rah ...?

| Do I have to change trains? Is there a connection for...? | *(pencil)* | ¿Tengo que hacer transbordo? ¿Hay correspondencia con...? |
| | *(speech)* | *Tehn'-goh keh ah-thehr' trans-baur'-doh? Ah'-y caur-res-paun-dehn'-the-ah caun ...?* |

| Does this train stop at ...? | *(pencil)* | ¿Para este tren en ...? |
| | *(speech)* | *Pah'-rah es'-teh trehn en ...?* |

| What time does it arrive at ...? | *(pencil)* | ¿A qué hora llega a ...? |
| | *(speech)* | *Ah keh' au'-rah lyeh'-gah ah ...?* |

| Is this seat vacant/occupied? | *(pencil)* | ¿Está libre/ocupado este asiento? |
| | *(speech)* | *Es-tah' lee'-breh/au-coo-pah'-doh es'-teh ah-se-en'-toh?* |

| Could you close the window, please? | *(pencil)* | ¿Puede cerrar la ventanilla, por favor? |
| | *(speech)* | *Poo-eh'-deh ther-rar' lah ven-tah-nee'-lyah, paur fah-vaur'?* |

| Which station is next? | *(pencil)* | ¿Cuál es la próxima estación? |
| | *(speech)* | *Coo-al' es lah prauc'-se-mah es-tah-the-aun'?* |

| We are running ten minutes late | *(pencil)* | Llevamos diez minutos de retraso |
| | *(speech)* | *Lyeh-vah'-mohs de-eth' me-noo'-tohs deh reh-trah'-soh* |

BY CAR

Road	Carretera	*Car-reh-teh'-rah*
Motorway	Autopista	*Ah-oo-tau-pees'-tah*
Dual carriage way	Autovía	*Ah-oo-tau-vee'-ah*
Main road	Carretera Nacional	*Car-reh-teh'-rah nah-the-au-nahl'*
Toll	Peaje	*Peh-ah'-heh*
Crossroads	Cruce	*Croo'-theh*
Level crossing	Paso a nivel	*Pah'-soh ah ne-vel'*
Dangerous bend	Curva peligrosa	*Coor'-vah peh-le-grau'-sah*
Diversion	Desviación	*Des-ve-ah-the-aun'*
Car	Coche	*Cau'-cheh*
Coach	Autocar	*AAh-oo-tau-car'*
Lorry	Camión	*Cah-me-aun'*
Bus	Autobús	*Ah-oo-tau-boos'*
Van	Furgoneta	*Foor-gau-neh'-tah*
Motorcycle	Moto	*Mau'-toh*
One-way street	Dirección única	*De-rec-the-aun' oo'-ne-cah*
Dead end	Calle sin salida	*Cah'-lyeh sin sah-lee'-dah*
Pedestrian crossing	Paso de peatones	*Pah'-soh deh peh-ah-tau'-nehs*
Road sign	Señal de tráfico	*Seh-nyahl' deh trah'-fe-coh*
Give way	Ceda el paso	*Theh'-dah el pah'-soh*
Roadworks	Obras	*Au'-brahs*
Speed limit	Límite de velocidad	*Lee'-me-teh deh veh-lau-the-dad'*
Driving licence	Permiso de conducir	*Per-mee'-soh deh caun-doo-theer'*

| The road to ..., please | Para ir a ..., por favor |
| | *Pah'-rah eer ah ..., paur fah-vaur'* |

| Is this the way to ...? | ¿Es ésta la carretera para ...? |
| | *Es es'-tah lah car-reh-teh'-rah pah'-rah ...?* |

| How far is ...? | ¿A qué distancia está ...? |
| | *Ah keh' dis-tahn'-the-ah es-tah' ...?* |

| It is not far. There are some ... kilometres | No está lejos. Hay unos ... kilómetros |
| | *Noh es-tah' leh'-hohs. Ah'-y oo'-nohs ... ki-lau'-meh-trohs* |

| Is the road good? | ¿Es buena la carretera? |
| | *Es boo-eh'-nah lah car-reh-teh'-rah?* |

| There are many bends | Hay muchas curvas |
| | *Ah'-y moo'-chahs coor'-vahs* |

| Where can I buy a road map? | ¿Dónde puedo comprar un mapa de carreteras? |
| | *Daun'-deh poo-eh'-doh caum-prar' oon mah'-pah deh car-reh-teh'-rahs?* |

| Which is the best road to get to the coast? | ¿Cuál es la mejor carretera para ir a la costa? |
| | *Coo-ahl' es lah meh-haur' car-reh-teh'-rah pah'-rah eer ah lah caus'-tah?* |

| How long does it take to get to ...? | ¿Cuánto tiempo se necesita para ir a ...? |
| | *Coo-ahn'-toh te-em'-poh seh neh-theh-see'-tah pah'-rah eer ah..?* |

Can you tell me how to get to the main road?	¿Puede indicarme qué dirección debo tomar para salir a la carretera nacional?
	Poo-eh'-deh in-de-car'-meh keh' de-rec-the-aun' deh'-boh tau-mar' pah'-rah sah-leer' ah lah car-reh-teh'-rah nah-the-au-nal'?
Can I park here?	¿Puedo aparcar aquí?
	Poo-eh'-doh ah-par-car' ah-kee'?
There is no parking place	No hay aparcamiento
	Noh ah'-y ah-par-cah-me-ehn'-toh

RENTING A CAR

I want to rent a car	Deseo alquilar un coche
	Deh-seh'-oh al-ke-lar' oon cau'-cheh
What is the cost per km. (per day)?	¿Cuál es el precio por kilómetro (por día)?
	Coo-ahl' es el preh'-the-oh paur ki-lau'-meh-troh (paur dee'-ah)?
For how many days?	¿Cuántos días?
	Coo-ahn'-tohs dee'-ahs?
Insurance included	Seguro incluido
	Seh-goo'-roh in-cloo-ee'-doh
It is ... euros plus V.A.T.	Son ... euros más I.V.A.
	Saun ... eh'-oo-ros mas ee'-vah

| Must I leave a deposit? | ✏️ | ¿Tengo que dejar un depósito? |
| | 💬 | *Tehn'-goh keh deh-har' oon deh-pau'-se-toh?* |

| Can I pay with a credit card? | ✏️ | ¿Puedo pagar con tarjeta? |
| | 💬 | *Poo-eh'-doh pah-gar' caun tar-heh'-tah?* |

BY CAR (SERVICES AND BREAKDOWNS)

Filling station	Gasolinera	*Gah-sau-le-neh'-rah*
Petrol	Gasolina	*Gah-sau-lee'-nah*
Air	Aire	*Ah'-y-reh*
Oil	Aceite	*Ah-theh'-y-teh*
Water	Agua	*Ah'-goo-ah*
Tank	Depósito	*Deh-pau'-se-toh*
Antifreeze	Anticongelante	*An-te-caun-heh-lahn'-teh*
Brake fluid	Líquido de frenos	*Lee'-ke-doh deh freh'-nohs*
Mechanic	Mecánico	*Meh-cah'-ne-coh*
Repair shop	Taller	*Tah-lyehr'*
Breakdown	Avería	*Ah-veh-ree'-ah*
Puncture	Pinchazo	*Pen-chah'-thoh*
Number-plate	Matrícula	*Mah-tree'-coo-lah*
Wing mirror	Retrovisor	*Re-trau-ve-saur'*
Exhaust-pipe	Tubo de escape	*Too'-boh deh es-cah'-peh*
Headlight	Faro	*Fah'-roh*
Indicator	Intermitente	*In-ter-me-tehn'-teh*
Rear-light	Piloto	*Pe-lau'-toh*

Bonnet	Capó	*Cah-pauh'*
Boot	Maletero	*Mah-leh-teh'-roh*
Door	Puerta	*Poo-er'-tah*
Windscreen	Parabrisas	*Pah-rah-bree'-sahs*
Window	Ventanilla	*Ven-tah-nee'-lyah*
Bumper	Parachoques	*Pah-rah-chau'-kehs*
Wheel	Rueda	*Roo-eh'-dah*
Tyre	Neumático	*Neh-oo-mah'-te-coh*
Spare wheel	Rueda de repuesto	*Roo-eh'-dah deh reh-poo-es'-toh*
Shock absorber	Amortiguador	*Ah-maur-te-goo-ah-daur'*
Engine	Motor	*Mau-taur'*
Starter motor	Estárter	*Es-tar'-ter*
Carburetor	Carburador	*Car-boo-rah-daur'*
Alternator	Alternador	*Al-ter-nah-daur'*
Mudguard	Guardabarros	*Goo-ar-dah-bar'-rohs*
Coil	Bobina	*Bau-bee'-nah*
Battery	Batería	*Bah-teh-ree'-ah*
Spark plug	Bujía	*Boo-hee'-ah*
Fuse	Fusible	*Foo-see'-bleh*
Piston	Pistón	*Pees-taun'*
Connecting rod	Biela	*Bee-eh'-lah*
Crankshaft	Cigüeñal	*The-goo-eh-nyahl'*
Cylinder head	Culata	*Coo-lah'-tah*
Cylinder head joint	Junta de culata	*Hoon'-tah deh coo-lah'-tah*
Crankcase	Cárter	*Car'-ter*
Fan belt	Correa de ventilador	*Caur-reh'-ah deh ven-te-lah-daur'*
Radiator	Radiador	*Rah-de-ah-daur'*
Jack	Gato	*Gah'-toh*

Set of tools	Herramientas	*Er-rah-me-ehn'-tahs*
Spare parts	Piezas de repuesto	*Pe-eh'-thas deh reh-poo-es'-toh*
Air (oil) filter	Filtro de aire (aceite)	*Feel'-troh deh ah'-e-rch (ah-theh'-y-teh)*
Gearbox	Caja de cambio	*Cah'-hah deh cahm'-be-oh*
Clutch	Embrague	*Em-brah'-gheh*
Steering-wheel	Volante	*Voh-lahn'-teh*
Ignition key	Llave de contacto	*Lyah'-veh deh caun-tac'-toh*
Gear lever	Palanca de cambio	*Pah-lahn'-cah deh cahm'-be-oh*
First, second, third gear	Primera, segunda, tercera (marcha)	*Pre-meh'-rah, seh-goon'-dah, ter-theh'-rah (mar'-chah)*
Footbrake	Pedal de freno	*Peh-dahl' deh freh'-noh*
Handbrake	Freno de mano	*Freh'-noh deh mah'-noh*
Accelerator pedal	Acelerador	*Ah-theh-leh-rah-daur'*
Reverse	Marcha atrás	*Mar'-chah ah-trahs'*

Is there a filling station near?	¿Hay una gasolinera cerca de aquí?
	Ah'-y oo'-nah gah-sau-le-neh'-rah thehr'-cah deh ah-kee'?

Fill her up, please	Lleno, por favor
	Lyeh'-noh, paur fah-vaur'

Put in twenty liters of unleaded petrol, please	Veinte litros de gasolina sin plomo, por favor
	Veh'-in-teh lee'-trohs deh gah-sau-lee'-nah sin plau'-moh, paur fah-vaur'

How much is it?	¿Cuánto es?
	Coo-an'-toh es?

I need some water	Necesito agua
	Neh-theh-see'-toh ah'-goo-ah
Examine the tyres	Revise los neumáticos
	Reh-vee'-seh lohs neh-oo-mah'-te-cohs
Please, give me a can of oil	Deme una lata de aceite, por favor
	Deh'-meh oo'-nah lah'-tah deh ah-theh'-e-teh, paur fah-vaur'
How long will it take to wash it?	¿Cuánto tardarán en lavarlo?
	Coo-an'-toh tahr-dah-rahn' en lah-var'-loh?
Where is a repair shop?	¿Dónde hay un taller?
	Daun'-deh ah'-y oon tah-lyer'?
My car has broken down ... kilometres from here	Mi coche se ha averiado a ... kilómetros de aquí
	Mee cau'-cheh seh ah ah-veh-re-ah'-doh ah ... ki-lau'-meh-trohs deh ah-kee'
Can you tow my car?	¿Pueden remolcar mi coche?
	Poo-eh'-den reh-maul-car' mee cau'-cheh?
What is the matter?	¿Qué le pasa?
	Keh' leh pah'-sah?
The battery is dead	La batería está descargada
	Lah bah-teh-ree'-ah es-tah' des-car-gah'-dah

The engine won't start	✏️	El motor no arranca
	💬	*El mau-taur' noh ar-rahn'-cah*

The radiator leaks	✏️	El radiador pierde
	💬	*El rah-de-ah-daur' pe-er'-deh*

Check the brakes	✏️	Revise los frenos
	💬	*Reh-vee'-seh lohs freh'-nohs*

The clutch does not work	✏️	No funciona el embrague
	💬	*Noh foon-the-au'-nah el em-brah'-gheh*

The fan belt is broken	✏️	La correa del ventilador está rota
	💬	*Lah caur-reh'-ah dehl ven-te-lah-daur' es-tah' rau'-tah*

The fuses are burned	✏️	Se han fundido los fusibles
	💬	*Seh ahn foon-dee'-doh lohs foo-see'-blehs*

Can you repair it temporarily?	✏️	¿Pueden hacer un arreglo provisional?
	💬	*Poo-eh'-den ah-thehr' oon ar-reh'-gloh prau-ve-se-au-nahl'?*

How long will it take to repair it?	✏️	¿Cuánto tardarán en arreglarlo?
	💬	*Coo-ahn'-toh tar-dah-rahn' en ar-reh-glar'-loh?*

Please, repair it as soon as possible	✏️	Por favor, repárelo lo antes posible
	💬	*Paur fah-vaur', reh-pah'-reh-loh lau ahn'-tes pau-see'-bleh*

We have to send for spare parts		Tenemos que pedir repuestos
		Teh-neh' mohs kch peh-deer' reh-poo-es'-tohs

It is already repaired		Ya está arreglado
		Yah es-tah' ar-reh-glah'-doh

Can you help me?		¿Puede Vd. ayudarme?
		Poo-eh'-deh oos-ted' ah-yoo-dar'-meh?

There has been an accident ... kilometres from here		Ha habido un accidente a ... kilómetros de aquí
		Ah ah-bee'-doh oon ac-the-dehn'-teh ah ... ki-lau'-meh-trohs deh ah-kee'

Where is the nearest hospital?		¿Dónde está el hospital más próximo?
		Daun'-deh es-tah' el aus-pe-tahl' mas prauc'-se-moh?

Please, telephone an ambulance		Por favor, llamen a una ambulancia
		Paur fah-vaur', lyah'-men ah oo'-nah am-boo-lahn'-the-ah

Here is my insurance cover (the car documents)		Aquí está mi póliza de seguros (los papeles del coche)
		Ah-kee' es-tah' mee pau'-le-thah deh seh-goo'-rohs (lohs pah-peh'-lehs dehl cau'-cheh)

Is there someone injured?		¿Hay algún herido?
		Ah'-y al-goon' eh-ree'-doh?

BY SHIP

Port	Puerto	Poo-er'-toh
Quay (dock)	Muelle	Moo-eh'-lyeh
Ship	Barco	Bar'-coh
Yacht	Yate	Yah'-teh
Ferry	Transbordador	Trans-baur-dah-daur'
Cruise ship	Transatlántico	Trans-at-lan'-te-coh
Deck	Cubierta	Coo-be-er'-tah
Deckchair	Hamaca	Ah-mah'-cah
Cabin	Camarote	Cah-mah-rau'-teh
Hold	Bodega	Bau-deh'-gah
Bow	Proa	Prau'-ah
Stern	Popa	Pau'-pah
Port side	Babor	Bah-baur'
Starboard	Estribor	Es-tre-baur'
Rudder	Timón	Te-maun'
Captain	Capitán	Cah-pe-tahn'
Steward	Camarero	Cah-mah-reh'-roh
Sailor	Marinero	Mah-re-neh'-roh
To heave up anchor	Levar anclas	Leh-var' ahn'-clas
To come alongside	Atracar	Ah-trah-car'
To call (at a port)	Hacer escala	Ah-ther' es-cah'-lah

Which way is it to the port?	¿Por dónde se va al puerto?
	Paur daun'-deh seh vah ahl poo-er'-toh?

I want a ticket for ...

Quiero un pasaje para ...

Ke-eh´-roh oon pah-sah´-heh pah´-rah ...?

On what day (at what time) does the ship sail?

¿Qué día (a qué hora) sale el barco?

Keh´ dee´-ah (ah keh´ au´-rah) sah´-leh el bar´-coh?

Is there a ship for ...?

¿Hay un barco para ...?

Ah´-y oon bar´-coh pah´-rah ...?

I'd like to book a sleeper/a cabin/a deck passenger ticket

Quisiera reservar una litera/ un camarote/un pasaje de cubierta

Ke-se-eh´-rah reh-ser-var´ oo´-nah le-teh´-rah/ oon cah-mah-rau´-teh/oon pah-sah´-heh deh coo-be-er´-tah

Give me a first class cabin

Deme un camarote de primera clase

Deh´-meh oon cah-mah-rau´-teh deh pre-meh´-rah clah´-seh

You must be at the port two hours before sailing

Debe estar en el puerto dos horas antes de la salida

Deh´-beh es-tar´ en el poo-er´-toh daus au´-rahs ahn´-tes deh lah sah-lee´-dah

Can you tell me the name of the ship?

¿Puede decirme el nombre del barco?

Poo-eh´-deh deh-theer´-meh el naum´-breh dehl bar´-coh?

How long is the crossing?

¿Cuánto dura la travesía?

Coo-an´-toh doo´-rah lah trah-veh-see´-ah?

| Can you give me a few labels for my luggage? | ¿Puede darme algunas etiquetas para el equipaje? |
| | *Poo-eh'-deh dar'-meh al-goo'-nahs eh-te-keh'-tas pah'-rah el eh-ke-pah'-heh?* |

| Which quay does the ship sail from? | ¿De qué muelle sale el barco? |
| | *Deh keh' moo-eh'-lyeh sah'-leh el bar'-coh?* |

| Which side is my cabin on? | ¿En qué lado está mi camarote? |
| | *En keh' lah'-doh es-tah' mee cah-mah-rau'-teh?* |

| This way, mind your head! | Por aquí, ¡cuidado con la cabeza! |
| | *Paur ah-kee', coo-e-dah'-doh caun lah cah-beh-thah!* |

| These parcels must travel in the baggage hold | Estos bultos tienen que ir en la bodega |
| | *Es'-tohs bool'-tohs te-eh'-nen keh eer en lah bau-deh'-gah* |

| How many ports do we call at? | ¿Cuántas escalas haremos? |
| | *Coo-ahn'-tahs es-cah'-lahs ah-reh'-mohs?* |

| Is there time to go ashore? | ¿Hay tiempo para desembarcar? |
| | *Ah'-y te-ehm'-poh pah'-rah deh-sem-bar-car'?* |

| We are coming into the harbour | Ya estamos entrando en el puerto |
| | *Yah es-tah'-mohs en-trahn'-doh en el poo-er'-toh* |

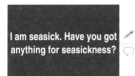

I am seasick. Have you got anything for seasickness?

Estoy mareado. ¿Tiene Vd. algo contra el mareo?

Es-toh'-y mah-reh-ah'-doh. Te-eh'-neh oos-ted' ahl'-goh caun'-trah el mah-reh'-oh?

MEANS OF TRANSPORT IN TOWN

Bus	Autobús	*Ah-oo-tau-boos'*
Underground	Metro	*Meh'-troh*
Taxi	Taxi	*Tac'-se*
Tram	Tranvía	*Tran-vee'-ah*
Ticket	Billete	*Be-lyeh'-teh*
Bus stop	Parada de autobús	*Pah-rah'-dah deh ah-oo-tau-boos'*
Way in/Entrance	Entrada	*En-trah'-dah*
Way out/Exit	Salida	*Sah-lee'-dah*
Request stop	Parada solicitada	*Pah-rah'-dah sau-le-the-tah'-dah*

I want to go to ...

Quiero ir a ...

Ke-eh'-roh eer ah ...

Which bus (tram) must I take for ...?

¿Qué autobús (tranvía) tengo que tomar para ir a ...?

Keh' ah-oo-tau-boos' (tran-vee'-ah) tehn'-goh keh tau-mar' pah'-rah eer ah ...?

Where does the number ... bus stop?	✎ ¿Dónde para el autobús número ...?
	💬 *Daun'-deh pah'-rah el ah-oo-tau-boos' noo'-meh-roh ...?*

Does this bus go to...?	✎ ¿Pasa este autobús por ...?
	💬 *Pah'-sah es'-teh ah-oo-tau-boos' paur ...?*

How often is the bus?	✎ ¿Con qué frecuencia pasa el autobús?
	💬 *Caun keh' freh-coo-ehn'-the-ah pah'-sah el ah-oo-tau-boos'?*

Which bus (underground) can I take to get to the railway station?	✎ ¿Qué autobús (metro) tengo que coger para ir a la estación de trenes?
	💬 *Keh' ah-oo-toh-boos' (meh'-troh) tehn'-goh keh cau-her' pah'-rah eer ah lah es-tah-the-aun' deh treh'-nehs?*

How much does it cost a single ticket?	✎ ¿Cuánto cuesta un billete de ida?
	💬 *Coo-ahn'-toh coo-es'-tah oon be-lyeh'-teh deh ee'-dah?*

Two tickets, please	✎ Dos billetes, por favor
	💬 *Daus be-lyeh'-tehs, paur fah-vaur'*

Where must I get off for...?	✎ ¿Dónde tengo que bajarme para ir a ...?
	💬 *Daun'-deh tehn'-goh keh bah-har'-meh pah'-rah eer ah ...?*

Is this seat occupied?	✎ ¿Está ocupado este asiento?
	💬 *Es-tah' au-coo-pah'-doh es'-teh ah-se-ehn'-toh?*

Where can I get a taxi?	✏	¿Dónde puedo encontrar un taxi?
	💬	*Daun´-deh poo-eh´-doh en-caun-trar´ oon tac´-se?*
How much does a taxi to the airport cost?	✏	¿Cuánto cuesta un taxi hasta el aeropuerto?
	💬	*Coo-ahn´-toh coo-es´-tah oon tac´-se as´-tah el ah-eh-rau-poo-er´-toh?*
How much is the fare for ...?	✏	¿Cuál es la tarifa para ...?
	💬	*Coo-ahl´ es lah tah-ree´-fah pah´-rah ...?*
Take me to ... street	✏	Lléveme a la calle ...
	💬	*Lyeh´-veh-meh ah lah cah´-lyeh ...*
Do you know where ... is?	✏	¿Sabe usted dónde está ...?
	💬	*Sah´-beh oos-ted´ daun-deh es-tah´ ...?*
Stop here, please	✏	Pare aquí, por favor
	💬	*Pah´-reh ah-kee´, paur fah-vaur´*
Can you wait a minute?	✏	¿Puede esperar un momento?
	💬	*Poo-eh´-deh es-peh-rar´ oon mau-mehn´-toh?*
Here you are	✏	Ya hemos llegado
	💬	*Yah eh´-mohs lyeh-gah´-doh*
How much is it?/ How much do I owe you?	✏	¿Cuánto es?/¿Cuánto le debo?
	💬	*Coo-ahn´-toh es?/Coo-ahn´-toh leh deh´-boh?*
Keep the change	✏	Quédese con la vuelta
	💬	*Keh´-deh-seh caun lah voo-el´-tah*

HOTELS

THE ARRIVAL

Hotel	Hotel	*Au-tehl'*
Guest-house	Pensión, hostal	*Pen-se-aun', aus-tahl'*
Hostel	Albergue	*Al-ber'-gheh*
Reception	Recepción	*Reh-cep-the-aun'*
Receptionist	Recepcionista	*Reh-cep-the-au-nees'-tah*
Manager	Gerente	*Heh-rehn'-teh*
Doorman	Portero	*Paur-teh'-roh*
Valet	Botones	*Bau-tau'-nes*
Chambermaid	Camarera	*Cah-mah-reh'-rah*
Guest	Huésped	*Oo-es'-ped*
Key	Llave	*Lyah'-veh*
Tip	Propina	*Prau-pee'-nah*
Low (high) season	Temporada baja (alta)	*Tem-pau-rah'-dah bah'-hah (al'-tah)*
Accommodation	Alojamiento	*Ah-lau-hah-me-ehn'-toh*
Stay	Estancia	*Es-tahn'-the-ah*
Lift	Ascensor	*As-then-saur'*
Floor	Piso (planta)	*Pee'-soh (plahn'-tah)*
Dining room	Comedor	*Cau-meh-daur'*
Bathroom	Cuarto de baño	*Coo-ar'-toh deh bah'-nyoh*
Heating	Calefacción	*Cah-leh-fac-the-aun'*
Air conditioning	Aire acondicionado	*Ah'-e-reh ah-caun-de-the-au-nah'-doh*

Nota: Parador = State run hotel in historic buildings

Single/double/ twin room	✎	Habitación individual/doble/ con dos camas
	💬	*Ah-be-tah-the-aun' in-de-vo-doo ahl'/dau'-blelı/ caun daus cah'-mahs*

Breakfast/half board/ full board	✎	Desayuno/media pensión/ pensión completa
	💬	*Deh-sah-yoo'-noh/meh'-de-ah pen-se-aun'/ pen-se-aun' caum-pleh'-tah*

Have you got any rooms?	✎	¿Tienen habitaciones libres?
	💬	*Te-eh'-nehn ah-be-tah-the-au'-nehs lee'-brehs?*

I have booked a room for ...	✎	Tengo reservada una habitación a nombre de ...
	💬	*Tehn'-goh reh-ser-vah'-dah oo'-nah ah-be-tah-the- aun' ah naum'-breh deh ...*

I want an outside (inside) room	✎	Desearía una habitación exterior (interior)
	💬	*Deh-seh-ah-ree'-ah oo'-nah ah-be-tah-the-aun' ex-teh-re-aur' (in-teh-re-aur')*

I would like a room facing the lake	✎	Quisiera una habitación con vistas al lago
	💬	*Ke-se-eh'-rah oo'-nah ah-be-tah-the-aun' caun vees'-tas ahl lah'-goh*

I want a room with a bath and telephone	✎	Quiero una habitación con baño y teléfono
	💬	*Ke-eh'-roh oo'-nah ah-be-tah-the-aun' caun bah'-nyoh ee teh-leh'-fau-noh*

Breakfast included?	✎	¿Incluido el desayuno?
	💬	*In-cloo-ee'-doh el deh-sah-yoo'-noh?*

How much is it?	✎	¿Cuál es el precio?
	💬	*Coo-ahl' es el preh'-the-oh?*

We have special prices for weekly stays	✎	Tenemos descuentos por estancias semanales
	💬	*Teh-neh'-mos des-coo-ehn'-tos paur es-tahn'-the-as seh-mah-nah'-lehs*

Your room is number... on the third floor, at the end of the corridor	✎	Su habitación es la número ... en la tercera planta, al fondo del pasillo
	💬	*Soo ah-be-tah-the-aun' es lah noo'-meh-roh ... en lah ter-theh'-rah plahn'-tah, ahl faun'-doh dehl pah-see'-lyoh*

May I see the room?	✎	¿Puedo ver la habitación?
	💬	*Poo-eh'-doh ver lah ah-be-tah-the-aun'?*

It is all right. I'll take it	✎	Está bien. Me quedo con ella
	💬	*Es-tah' be-en'. Meh keh'-doh caun eh'-lyah*

It is too small. Have you got another room bigger?	✎	Es demasiado pequeña. ¿No tienen otra más amplia?
	💬	*Es deh-mah-se-ah'-doh peh-keh'-nyah. Noh te-eh'-nehn au'-trah mas ahm'-ple-ah?*

You have to fill in the hotel registration form	✎	Tiene usted que rellenar la hoja de registro
	💬	*Te-eh'-neh oos-ted' keh reh-lyeh-nar' lah au'-hah deh reh-hees'-troh*

How long will you be staying?	✎	¿Cuánto tiempo piensa quedarse?
	💬	*Coo-ahn'-toh te-ehm'-poh pe-ehn'-sah keh-kdar'-seh?*

About five days	✎	Unos cinco días
	💬	*Oo'-nohs thin'-coh dee'-ahs*

	Send up my luggage, please	✏️	Súbanme el equipaje, por favor

Send up my luggage, please
✏️ Súbanme el equipaje, por favor
💬 *Soo'-ban-meh el eh-ke-pah'-heh, paur fah-vaur'*

At what time is breakfast served?
✏️ ¿A qué hora se sirve el desayuno?
💬 *Ah keh' au'-rah seh seer'-veh el deh-sah-yoo'-noh?*

Please, wake me at seven
✏️ Haga el favor de despertarme a las siete
💬 *Ah'-gah el fah-vaur' deh des-per-tar'-meh ah lahs se-eh'-teh*

YOUR STAY

Bed	Cama	*Cah'-mah*
Mattress	Colchón	*Caul-chaun'*
Pillow	Almohada	*Al-moh-ah'-dah*
Blanket	Manta	*Mahn'-tah*
Sheets	Sábanas	*Sah'-bah-nas*
Tap	Grifo	*Gree'-foh*
Switch	Interruptor	*In-ter-roop-taur'*
Towel	Toalla	*Tau-ah'-lyah*
Soap	Jabón	*Hah-baun'*
Glass	Vaso	*Vah'-soh*
Ashtray	Cenicero	*Theh-ne-theh'-roh*
Claim	Queja	*Keh'-hah*
Do not disturb	No molestar	*Noh mau-les-tar'*
For the laundry	Para lavar	*Pah'-rah lah-var'*

My key, please, number ...	✏ Mi llave, por favor, número ...	
	💬 *Mee lyah'-veh, paur fah-vaur', noo'-meh-roh ...*	

Serve my breakfast in my room	✏ Súbanme el desayuno a la habitación	
	💬 *Soo'-ban-meh el deh-sah-yoo'-noh ah lah ah-be-tah-the-aun'*	

THE BREAKFAST

Coffee	Café	*Cah-feh'*
Tea	Té	*Teh*
Milk	Leche	*Leh'-cheh*
Chocolate	Chocolate	*Choh-cau-lah'-teh*
Bread	Pan	*Pahn*
Butter	Mantequilla	*Man-teh-kee'-lyah*
Yoghurt	Yogur	*Yoh-goor'*
Egg	Huevo	*Oo-eh'-voh*
Toast	Tostada	*Taus-tah'-dah*
Jam	Mermelada	*Mer-meh-lah'-dah*
Marmalade	Mermelada de naranja	*Mer-meh-lah'-dah deh nah-rahn'-hah*
Honey	Miel	*Me-ehl'*
Corn flakes	Cereales	*The-reh-ah'-lehs*
Orange juice	Zumo de naranja	*Thoo'-moh deh nah-rahn'-hah*
Ham and eggs	Huevos con jamón	*Oo-eh'-vohs caun hah-maun'*
Fried eggs	Huevos fritos	*Oo-eh'-vohs free'-tohs*

83

| May I have something to eat now? | ✏️ | ¿Podría tomar algo a esta hora? |
| | 💬 | *Pau-dree'-ah tau-mar' ahl'-goh ah es'-tah au'-rah?* |

| The dining room is closed | ✏️ | El comedor está cerrado |
| | 💬 | *El cau-meh-daur' es-tah' ther-rah'-doh* |

| Put it on my bill. Room number ... | ✏️ | Cárguelo en mi cuenta. Habitación número ... |
| | 💬 | *Car'-gheh-loh en mee coo-ehn'-tah. Ah-be-tah-the-aun' noo'-meh-roh ...* |

| Please, iron these trousers | ✏️ | Por favor, pláncheme estos pantalones |
| | 💬 | *Paur fah-vaur', plahn'-cheh-meh es'-tohs pan-tah-lau'-nehs* |

| Are there any letters for me? | ✏️ | ¿Hay cartas para mí? |
| | 💬 | *Ah'-y car'-tahs pah'-rah mee?* |

| Have you got a street plan? | ✏️ | ¿Tienen un plano de la ciudad? |
| | 💬 | *Te-eh'-nen oon plah'-noh deh lah the-oo-dad'?* |

| Where is the telephone directory? | ✏️ | ¿Dónde está la guía telefónica? |
| | 💬 | *Daun'-deh es-tah' lah ghee'-ah teh-leh-fau'-ne-cah* |

| I want to make a telephone call | ✏️ | Deseo hacer una llamada |
| | 💬 | *Deh-seh'-oh ah-thehr' oo'-nah lyah-mah'-dah* |

| The switch in the bathroom does not work properly | ✏️ | El interruptor del cuarto de baño no funciona bien |
| | 💬 | *El in-ter-roop-taur' dehl coo-ar'-toh deh bah'-nyoh noh foon-the-au'-nah be-en'* |

The water is cold	El agua está fría
	El ah'-goo-ah es-tah' free'-ah

Where can I post these letters?	¿Dónde puedo echar estas cartas?
	Daun'-deh poo-eh'-doh eh-char' es'-tahs car'-tahs?

Please, send for a taxi	Pídame un taxi, por favor
	Pee'-dah-meh oon tac'-se, paur fah-vaur'

I want a guide who speaks English	Quiero un guía que hable inglés
	Ke-eh'-roh oon ghee'-ah keh ah'-bleh in-gles'

I want to rent a car	Quiero alquilar un coche
	Ke-eh'-roh al-ke-lar' oon cau'-cheh

Is there a garage in the hotel?	¿Hay garaje en el hotel?
	Ah'-y gah-rah'-heh en el au-tehl'?

YOUR DEPARTURE

We are leaving on ...	Nos vamos el ... *Naus vah'-mohs el ...*
Could you make out my bill?	¿Quiere prepararme la cuenta? *Ke-eh'-reh preh-pah-rar'-meh lah coo-ehn'-tah?*
I think there is a mistake. Please check it	Creo que se han equivocado. Repásela, por favor *Creh'-oh keh seh ahn eh-ke-vou-cah'-doh. Reh-pah'-seh-lah, paur fah-vaur'*
Is everything included?	¿Está todo incluido? *Es-tah' tau'-doh in-cloo-ee'-doh?*
Could I leave these things here until midday?	¿Puedo dejar estas cosas aquí hasta mediodía? *Poo-eh'-doh deh-har' es'-tahs cau'-sahs ah-kee' as'-tah meh-de-au-dee'-ah?*
Send down my luggage, please	Bájenme las maletas, por favor *Bah'-hen-meh lahs mah-leh'-tahs, paur fah-vaur'*
Have a good journey!	¡Buen viaje! *Boo-en' ve-ah'-heh!*
Thank you very much for everything	Muchas gracias por todo *Moo'-chahs grah'-the-ahs paur tau'-doh*

BARS AND RESTAURANTS

BARS AND RESTAURANTS

| Is there a bar near here? | ✎ ¿Hay un bar cerca de aquí? |
| | 💬 *Ah'-y oon bar thehr'-cah deh ah-kee'?* |

| Can you suggest a bar where you can get something to eat? | ✎ ¿Puede indicarme un bar donde se pueda comer algo? |
| | 💬 *Poo-eh'-deh in-de-car'-meh oon bar daun'-deh seh poo-eh'-dah cau-mer' ahl'-goh?* |

| Can you make me a sandwich? | ✎ ¿Puede hacerme un bocadillo? |
| | 💬 *Poo-eh'-deh ah-thehr'-meh oon bau-cah-dee'-lyoh?* |

| Have you got any hot dishes? | ✎ ¿Tienen platos calientes? |
| | 💬 *Te-eh'-nen plah'-tohs cah-le-ehn'-tehs?* |

| What kind of ... have you got? | ✎ ¿Qué tipo de ... tienen? |
| | 💬 *Keh' tee'-poh deh ... te-eh'-nen?* |

| We have "tapas" (small dishes of food) | ✎ Tenemos tapas |
| | 💬 *Teh-neh'-mohs tah'-pahs* |

"TAPAS"

Croquette	Croqueta	*Crau-keh'-tah*
Small brochette	Pinchito	*Pin-chee'-toh*
Stuffed eggs	Huevos rellenos	*Oo-eh'-vohs reh-lyeh'-nohs*
Tripe	Callos	*Cah'-lyohs*
Meat-ball	Albóndiga	*Al-baun'-de-gah*
Potato omelet	Tortilla de patatas	*Taur-tee'-lyah deh pah-tah'-tahs*

89

Can we sit at this table?	¿Podemos sentarnos en esta mesa?
	au-deh'-mos sen-tar'-nos en es'-tah meh'-sah?
Could you bring us another ...?	¿Puede traernos otro/a ...?
	Poo-eh'-deh trah-er'-nos au'-troh/ah ...?
Have you got a telephone?	¿Tienen teléfono?
	Te-eh'-nen teh-leh'-fau-noh?
Where is the toilet?	¿Dónde están los servicios?
	Daun'-deh es-tahn' lohs ser-vee'-the-ohs?
The bill, please	La cuenta, por favor
	Lah coo-ehn'-tah, paur fah-vaur'
How much is it?	¿Cuánto es?
	Coo-ahn'-toh es?
I would like a/an ...	Quiero un/una ...
	Ke-eh'-roh oon/oo'-nah ...

BEBIDAS

White coffee	Café con leche	*Cah-feh' caun leh'-cheh*
Black coffee	Café solo	*Cah-feh' sau'-loh*
Orange juice	Zumo de naranja	*Thoo'-moh deh nah-ran'-hah*
Cold/ hot milk	Leche fría/caliente	*Leh'-cheh free'-ah/cah-le-ehn'-teh*
Tea with lemon (milk)	Té con limón (leche)	*Teh caun le-maun' (leh'-cheh)*
Hot chocolate	Chocolate caliente	*Chau-cau-lah'-teh cah-le-ehn'-teh*
Mineral water (still, sparkling)	Agua mineral (con/sin gas)	*Ah'-goo-ah me-neh-rahl' (caun/sin gahs)*

Beer	Cerveza	*Ther-veh'-thah*
Draft beer	Caña	*Cah'-nyah*
Pint	Jarra	*Har'-rah*

| A glass of .... | ✏️ | Un vaso de ... |
| | 💬 | *Oon vah'-soh deh ...* |

| A cup of ... | ✏️ | Una taza de ... |
| | 💬 | *Oo'-nah tah'-thah deh ...* |

THE TABLE

Table	Mesa	*Meh'-sah*
Chair	Silla	*See'-lyah*
Tablecloth	Mantel	*Man-tehl'*
Serviette	Servilleta	*Ser-ve-lyeh'-tah*
Dish	Plato	*Plah'-toh*
Spoon	Cuchara	*Coo-chah'-rah*
Fork	Tenedor	*Teh-neh-daur'*
Knife	Cuchillo	*Coo-chee'-lyoh*
Dessert spoon	Cucharilla	*Coo-chah-ree'- lyah*
Glass	Vaso	*Vah'-soh*
(Wine) glass	Copa	*Cau'-pah*
Cup	Taza	*Tah'-thah*
Waiter	Camarero	*Cah-mah-reh'-roh*
Head waiter	Maitre	*Metr*
Tip	Propina	*Prau-pee'-nah*

Can you suggest a restaurant for local cuisine?	¿Puede recomendarme un restaurante típico?
	Poo-eh'-deh reh-cau-men-dar'-meh oon res-tah-oo-rahn'-teh tee'-pe-coh?

A table for two, please	Una mesa para dos, por favor
	Oo'-nah meh'-sah pah'-rah daus, paur fah-vaur'

I would like to book a table for ... people for ...	Quisiera reservar una mesa para ... personas ... para las ...
	Ke-se-eh'-rah reh-ser-var' oo'-nah meh'-sah pah'-rah ... per-sau'-nahs pah'-rah lahs ...

Could we have ...	¿Podemos tener ...
	Pau-deh'-mohs teh-ner' ...

a table near the window?	una mesa cerca de la ventana?
	oo'-nah meh'-sah thehr'-cah deh lah ven-tah'-nah?

a quiet table?	una mesa tranquila?
	oo'-nah meh'-sah tran-kee'-lah?

a table away from the door?	una mesa lejos de la puerta?
	oo'-nah meh'-sah leh'-hohs deh lah poo-er'-tah?

Is this table reserved?	¿Está reservada esta mesa?
	Es-tah' reh-ser-vah'-dah es'-tah meh'-sah?

| Where can we sit? | ¿Dónde podemos sentarnos? |
| | *Daun'-deh pau-deh'-mohs sen-tar'-nohs?* |

| I am waiting for some friends | Estoy esperando a unos amigos |
| | *Es-tau'-y es-peh-rahn'-doh ah oo'-nos ah-mee'-gohs* |

| Could you bring me an aperitif? | ¿Puede traerme un aperitivo? |
| | *Poo-eh'-deh trah-er'-meh oon ah-peh-re-tee'-voh?* |

| Can you bring me the menu? | ¿Puede traerme la carta? |
| | *Poo-eh'-deh trah-er'-meh lah car'-tah?* |

| Have you got a wine list? | ¿Tiene una carta de vinos? |
| | *Te-eh'-neh oo'-nah car'-tah deh vee'-nohs?* |

| Could you suggest something special? | ¿Puede recomendarme algo especial? |
| | *Poo-eh'-deh reh-cau-men-dar'-meh ahl'-goh es-peh-the-ahl'?* |

| What is the local speciality? | ¿Cuál es la especialidad de la casa? |
| | *Coo-ahl' es lah es-peh-the-ah-le-dad' deh lah cah'-sah?* |

| Which wine do you recommend? | ¿Qué vino me recomienda? |
| | *Keh' vee'-noh meh reh-cau-me-ehn'-dah?* |

| What are the ingredients of this dish? | ¿Cuáles son los ingredientes de este plato? |
| | *Coo-ah'-lehs saun lohs in-greh-de-ehn'-tehs deh es'-teh plah'-toh?* |

What would you like?	¿Qué les sirvo?	*Keh' lehs seer'-voh?*
Bring me (us) ...	Tráigame (tráiganos) ...	*Trah'-e-gah-meh (trah'-e-gah-nohs) ...*
First of all, ...	De primero, ...	*Deh pre-meh'-roh,...*
Afterwards, ...	De segundo, ...	*Deh seh-goon'-doh, ...*
The same for me	Lo mismo para mí	*Lau mees'-moh pah'-rah mee*
Enough, thanks	Está bien, gracias	*Es-tah' be-en', grah'-the-ahs*
More, please	Más, por favor	*Mas, paur fah-vaur'*
Can I have ...	¿Puede traerme ...	*Poo-eh'-deh trah-er'-meh ...*
another glass	otro vaso	*au'-troh vah'-soh*
some more bread	más pan	*mas pahn*

salt and pepper	sal y pimienta
	sahl ee pe-me- ehn'-tah

This dish is cold. Could you heat it for me?	Esta comida está fría. ¿Puede calentármela?
	Es'-tah cau-mee'-dah es-tah' free'-ah. Poo-eh'-deh cah-len-tar'-meh-lah?

This dish is underdone. Could you cook it a little more?	Esta comida está poco hecha. ¿Pueden pasarla un poco más?
	Es'-tah cau-mee'-dah es-tah' pau'-coh eh'-chah. Poo-eh'-den pah-sar'-lah oon pau'-coh mas?

What is there for dessert?	¿Qué tienen de postre?
	Keh' te-eh'-nen deh paus'-treh?

Will you have a coffee?	¿Tomarán café?
	Tau-mah-rahn' cah-feh'?

The bill, please	La cuenta, por favor
	Lah coo-ehn'-tah, paur fah-vaur'

Do you accept credit cards?	¿Puedo pagar con tarjeta?
	Poo-eh'-doh pah-gar' caun tar-heh'-tah?

I need the receipt	Necesito la factura
	Neh-theh-see'-toh lah fac-too'-rah

| Keep the change | | Quédese con la vuelta |
| | | *Keh'-deh-seh caun lah voo-el'-tah* |

| Have you got a lighter/light, please | | Por favor, ¿me da fuego? |
| | | *Paur fah-vaur', meh dah foo-eh'-goh?* |

COOKING TERMS

Fried	Frito	*Free'-toh*
Boiled	Hervido	*Er-vee'-doh*
Roast(ed)	Asado	*Ah-sah'-doh*
Grilled	A la plancha	*A lah plahn'-chah*
Toasted	Tostado	*Taus-tah'-doh*
Baked	Al horno	*Ahl aur'-noh*
Hot	Picante	*Pe-can'-teh*
Raw	Crudo	*Croo'-doh*
Sour	Agrio	*Ah'-gre-oh*
Smoked	Ahumado	*Ah-oo-mah'-doh*
Salty	Salado	*Sah-ah'-doh*
Unsalted	Soso	*Sau'-soh*
Rare (underdone)	Poco hecho	*Pau'-coh eh'-choh*
Medium	Medio	*Meh'-de-oh*
Well done	Muy hecho	*Moo'-y eh'-choh*

CONDIMENTS

Salt	Sal	*Sahl*
Pepper	Pimienta	*Pe-me-ehn'-tah*
Spice	Especia	*Es-peh'-the-ah*
Oil	Aceite	*Ah-the'-e-teh*
Vinegar	Vinagre	*Ve-nah'-greh*
Sauce	Salsa	*Sahl'-sah*
Mustard	Mostaza	*Maus-tah'-thah*
Mayonnaise	Mayonesa	*Mah-yoh-neh'-sah*
Paprika	Pimentón	*Pe-men-taun'*

HORS D'OEUVRES

Butter	Mantequilla	*Man-teh-kee'-lyah*
Bread	Pan	*Pahn*
Olives	Aceitunas	*Ah-thei-too'-nahs*
Cheese	Queso	*Keh'-soh*
Ham	Jamón	*Hah-maun'*
Cooked meats	Embutidos	*Em-boo-tee'-dohs*

EGGS

Fried	Frito	*Free'-toh*
Soft-boiled	Pasado por agua	*Pah-sah'-doh paur ah'-goo-ah*
Hard-boiled	Duro	*Doo'-roh*
Scrambled	Revuelto	*Reh-voo-ehl'-toh*
Omelet	Tortilla	*Taur-tee'-lyah*

MEAT

Veal	Ternera	*Ter-neh'-rah*
Pork	Cerdo	*Thehr'-doh*
Lamb	Cordero	*Caur-deh'-roh*
Chicken	Pollo	*Pau'-lyoh*

Turkey	Pavo	*Pah'-voh*
Rabbit	Conejo	*Cau-neh'-hoh*
Liver	Hígado	*Ee'-gah-doh*
Kidneys	Riñones	*Re-nyau'-nehs*
Loin	Lomo	*Lau'-moh*
Mince	Carne picada	*Car'-neh pe-cah'-dah*
Chop	Chuleta	*Choo-leh'-tah*
Rib	Costilla	*Caus-tee'-lyah*
Steak	Filete	*Fe-leh'-teh*
Sirloin	Solomillo	*Sau-lau-mee'-lyoh*
Entrecot	Entrecot	*En-treh-caut'*

FISH AND SEAFOOD

Sardine	Sardina	*Sar-dee'-nah*
Anchovy	Boquerón	*Bau-keh-raun'*
Tuna	Atún	*Ah-toon'*
Sole	Lenguado	*Len-goo-ah'-doh*
Hake	Merluza	*Mer-loo'-thah*
Cod	Bacalao	*Bah-cah-lah'-oh*
Salmon	Salmón	*Sal-maun'*
Red mullet	Salmonete	*Sal-mau-neh'-teh*
Swordfish	Pez espada	*Peth es-pah'-dah*
Sea bream	Besugo	*Beh-soo'-goh*
Trout	Trucha	*Troo'-chah*
Schrimp	Gamba	*Gahm'-bah*
Prawn	Langostino	*Lan-gaus-tee'-noh*
Lobster	Langosta	*Lan-gaus'-tah*
Squid	Calamar	*Cah-lah-mar'*

Octopus	Pulpo	*Pool'-poh*
Crab	Cangrejo	*Can-greh'-hoh*
Mussel	Mejillón	*Meh-he-lyaun'*
Oyster	Ostra	*Aus'-trah*
Clam	Almeja	*Al-meh'-hah*

VEGETABLES

Lettuce	Lechuga	*Leh-choo'-gah*
Tomato	Tomate	*Tau-mah'-teh*
Potato	Patata	*Pah-tah'-tah*
Cucumber	Pepino	*Peh-pee'-noh*
Onion	Cebolla	*Theh-bau'-lyah*
Garlic	Ajo	*Ah'-hoh*
(Green, red) pepper	Pimiento	*Pe-me-en'-toh*
Carrot	Zanahoria	*Thah-nah-au'-re-ah*
Spinach	Espinaca	*Es-pe-nah'-cah*
Asparagus	Espárrago	*Es-par'-rah-goh*
Aubergine	Berenjena	*Beh-ren-heh'-nah*
Mushroom	Seta	*Seh'-tah*
Artichoke	Alcachofa	*Al-cah-chau'-fah*
Cabbage	Col	*Caul*
Cauliflower	Coliflor	*Cau-le-flaur'*
Green beans	Judías verdes	*Hoo-dee'-ahs ver'-dehs*
Celery	Apio	*Ah'-pe-oh*
Leek	Puerro	*Poo-er'-roh*
Peas	Guisantes	*Ghee-sahn'-tehs*
Sweet corn	Maíz	*Mah-eeth'*
Endive	Endivia	*En-dee'-ve-ah*

FRUITS AND DESSERTS

Orange	Naranja	*Nah-rahn'-huah*
Lemon	Limón	*Le-maun'*
Grapefruit	Pomelo	*Pau-meh'-loh*
Apple	Manzana	*Man-thah'-nah*
Pear	Pera	*Peh'-rah*
Peach	Melocotón	*Meh-lau-cau- taun'*
Plum	Ciruela	*The-roo-eh'-lah*
Apricot	Albaricoque	*Al-bah-re-cau'-keh*
Cherry	Cereza	*Theh-reh'-thah*
Strawberry	Fresa	*Freh'-sah*
Grape	Uva	*Oo'-vah*
Banana	Plátano	*Plah'-tah-noh*
Melon	Melón	*Meh-laun'*
Watermelon	Sandía	*San-dee'-ah*
Pineapple	Piña	*Pee'-nyah*
Yoghurt	Yogur	*Yau-goor'*
Ice cream	Helado	*Eh-lah'-doh*
Caramel custard	Flan	*Flahn*
Cream	Nata	*Nah'-tah*
Cake	Tarta	*Tar'-tah*
Cheese	Queso	*Keh'-soh*
Fruit salad	Macedonia de frutas	*Mah-theh-dau'-ne-ah deh froo'-tahs*
Rice pudding	Arroz con leche	*Ar-rauth' caun leh'-cheh*
Apple pie	Tarta de manzana	*Tar'-tah deh man-thah'-nah*
Custard	Natillas	*Nah-tee'-lyahs*

DRINKS

Water	Agua	*Ah'-goo-ah*
Lemonade	Gaseosa	*Gah-seh-au'-sah*
Wine	Vino	*Vee'-noh*
White	Blanco	*Blahn'-coh*
Red	Tinto	*Tin'-toh*
Rosé	Rosado	*Rau-sah'-doh*
Dry	Seco	*Seh'-coh*
Sweet	Dulce	*Dool'-theh*
Vintage	Cosecha	*Cau-seh'-chah*
Champagne	Champán	*Chahm-pahn'*
Liqueur	Licor	*Le-caur'*
Whisky	Whisky	*Goo-is'-kee*
Rum	Ron	*Raun*
Gin	Ginebra	*He-neh'-brah*
Brandy	Coñac	*Cau-nyac'*

DISHES

Mixt salad	Ensalada mixta	*En-sah-lah'-dah mix'-tah*
Gazpacho (*)	Gazpacho	*Gath-pah'-choh*
Paella (**)	Paella	*Pah-eh'-lyah*
Omelet (***)	Tortilla	*Taur-tee'-lyah*
Consomme	Consomé	*Caun-sau-meh'*
Stew	Estofado	*Es-tau-fah'-doh*

(*) **Gazpacho** (vegetable cold soup)
(**) **Paella** (rice, meat, fish, vegetables and saffron)
(***) **Tortilla a la francesa** (plain omelet)
      Tortilla a la española (potato omelet)

Roast chicken	Pollo asado	*Pau'-lyoh ah-sah'-doh*
Vegetable soup	Sopa de verduras	*Suu'-pah deh ver- doo'-rahs*
Fish soup	Sopa de pescado	*Sau'-pah deh pes-cah'-doh*
Pork chops	Chuletas de cerdo	*Choo-leh'-tahs deh thehr'-doh*
Lamb chops	Chuletas de cordero	*Choo-leh'-tahs deh caur-deh'-roh*
Pepper steack	Solomillo a la pimienta	*Sau-lau-mee'-lyoh ah lah pe-me-ehn'-tah*
Veal steak	Filete de ternera	*Fe-leh'-teh deh ter-neh'-rah*
Hake	Merluza	*Mer-loo'-thah*
Romaine	a la romana	*ah lah rau-mah'-nah*
Trout with almonds	Trucha con almendras	*Troo'-chah caun al-men'-drahs*
Baked sea bream	Besugo al horno	*Beh-soo'-goh ahl aur'-noh*

SHOPPING

SHOPS

Bookshop	Librería	Le-breh-ree'-ah
Baker's	Panadería	Pah-nah-deh-ree'-ah
Butcher's	Carnicería	Car-ne-theh-ree'-ah
Cakeshop	Pastelería	Pas-teh-leh-ree'-ah
Chemist's	Farmacia	Far-mah'-the-ah
Delicatessen	Charcutería	Char-coo-teh-ree'-ah
Department store	Grandes almacenes	Gran'-des al-mah-theh'-nehs
Dry cleaning	Tintorería	Teen-tau-reh-ree'-ah
Florist's	Floristería	Flau-res-teh-ree'-ah
Greengrocer's	Frutería	Froo-teh-ree'-ah
Fishshop	Pescadería	Pes-cah-deh-ree'-ah
Hair dresser's	Peluquería	Peh-loo-keh-ree'-ah
Herbalist shop	Herboristería	Er-bau-res-teh-ree'-ah
Ironmonger's	Ferretería	Fer-reh-teh-ree'-ah
Jeweller's	Joyería	Hau-yeh-ree'-ah
Laundry	Lavandería	Lah-van-deh-ree'-ah
Market	Mercado	Mer-cah'-doh
Newsagent's	Quiosco	Ke-aus'-coh
Perfumery	Perfumería	Per-foo-meh-ree'-ah
Photographic shop	Tienda de fotos	Te-ehn'-dah deh fau'-tohs
Optician's	Óptica	Aup'-te-cah
Shoeshop	Zapatería	Thah-pah-teh-ree'-ah
Supermarket	Supermercado	Soo-per-mer-cah'-doh
Tobacconist's	Estanco	Es-tahn'-coh
Antique shop	Antigüedades	An-te-goo-eh-dah'-dehs
Handicraft	Artesanía	Ar-teh-sah-nee'-ah
Souvenir	Recuerdo	Reh-coo-er'-doh

Open	Abierto	*Ah-be-er'-toh*
Closed	Cerrado	*Ther-rah'-doh*
Cashdesk	Caja	*Cah'-hah*
Entrance	Entrada	*En-trah'-dah*
Exit	Salida	*Sah-lee'-dah*
Pull	Tirar	*Te-rar'*
Push	Empujar	*Em-poo-har'*
Shop window	Escaparate	*Es-cah-pah-rah'-teh*
Counter	Mostrador	*Maus-trah-daur'*
Shop assistant	Dependiente/a	*Deh-pen-de-ehn'-teh/tah*
Fire exit	Salida de emergencia	*Sah-lee'-dah deh eh-mer-hehn'-the-ah*
Cheques not accepted	No se admiten cheques	*Noh seh ad-mee'-ten cheh'-kehs*
Complaint book	Libro de reclamaciones	*Lee'-broh deh reh-clah-mah-the-au'-nehs*

AT THE BOOKSHOP-NEWSAGENT'S 📖

Book	Libro	*Lee'-broh*
Dictionary	Diccionario	*Dic-the-au-nah-re-oh*
Novel	Novela	*Nau-veh'-lah*
Postcard	Postal	*Paus-tahl'*
Newspaper	Periódico	*Peh-re-au'-de-coh*
Magazine	Revista	*Reh-vees'-tah*
Ball point pen	Bolígrafo	*Bau-lee'-grah-foh*
Pen	Pluma	*Ploo'-mah*
Pencil	Lápiz	*Lah'-pith*

Marker pen	Rotulador	*Rau-too-lah-daur'*
Envelope	Sobre	*Sau'-breh*
Writing paper	Papel de carta	*Pah-pehl' deh car'-tah*
Guide	Guía	*Ghee'-ah*
Map	Mapa	*Mah'-pah*
Plan	Plano	*Plah'-noh*

Give me...	✏	Deme...
	💬	*Deh'-meh...*

I would like...	✏	Quería (quisiera)...
	💬	*Keh-ree'-ah (ke-se-eh'-rah)...*

I am looking for a book by... / on... Can you help me?	✏	Estoy buscando un libro de... / sobre... ¿Puede ayudarme?
	💬	*Es-tau'-y boos-cahn'-doh oon lee'-broh deh.../ sau'-breh ... Poo-eh'-deh ah-yoo-dar'-meh?*

I would like a book concerning the history and art of this city	✏	Quisiera un libro sobre la historia y el arte de esta ciudad
	💬	*Ke-se-eh'-rah oon lee'-broh sau'-breh lah is-tau'-re-ah ee el ar'-teh deh es'-tah the-oo-dad'*

Is it translated into English?	✏	¿Está traducido al inglés?
	💬	*Es-tah' trah-doo-thee'-doh ahl in-gles'?*

Where can I buy a road map?	✏	¿Dónde puedo comprar un mapa de carreteras?
	💬	*Daun'-deh poo-eh'-doh caum-prar' oon mah'-pah deh car-reh-teh'-rahs?*

Have you got English newspapers/magazines/books?		¿Tiene periódicos/revistas/libros ingleses?
		Te-eh'-neh peh-re-au'-de-cohs/reh-vees'-tahs/ lee'-brohs in-gleh'-sehs?

AT THE CHEMIST'S

Prescription	Receta	*Reh-theh'-tah*
Tablet	Pastilla	*Pas-tee'-lyah*
Pill	Píldora	*Peel'-dau-rah*
Cough mixture	Jarabe	*Hah-rah'-beh*
Cream	Pomada	*Pau-mah'-dah*
Suppository	Supositorio	*Soo-pau-se-tau'-re-oh*
Laxative	Laxante	*Lac-sahn'-teh*
Sedative	Calmante	*Cal-mahn'-telı*
Injection	Inyección	*In-yec-the-aun'*
Bandage	Venda	*Vehn'-dah*
Sticking plasters	Tiritas	*Te-ree'-tahs*
Cotton wool	Algodón	*Al-gau-daun'*
Gauze	Gasa	*Gah'-sah*
Alcohol	Alcohol	*Al-cau-aul'*
Thermometer	Termómetro	*Ter-mau'-meh- troh*
Sanitary towels	Compresas	*Caum-preh'-sahs*

Napkins	Pañales	*Pah-nyah-lehs'*
Toothpaste	Pasta de dientes	*Pas'-tah deh de-ehn'-tehs*
Toothbrush	Cepillo de dientes	*Theh-pee'-lyoh deh de-ehn'-tehs*
Paper tissues	Pañuelos de papel	*Pah-nyoo-eh'-lohs deh pah-pehl'*
Duty	Farmacia	*Far-mah'-the-ah*
chemist	de guardia	*deh goo-ar'-de-ah*

Could you give me something for...?	🖉	¿Puede darme algo contra...?
	💬	*Poo-eh'-deh dar'-meh ahl'-goh caun'-trah...?*

Fever	Fiebre	*Fe-eh'-breh*
Cold	Resfriado	*Res-fre-ah'-doh*
Cough	Tos	*Taus*
Headache	Dolor de cabeza	*Dau-laur' deh cah-beh'-thah*
Toothache	Dolor de muelas	*Dau-laur' deh moo-eh'-lahs*
Diarrhoea	Diarrea	*De-ar-reh'-ah*
Constipation	Estreñimiento	*Es-treh-nye-me-ehn'-toh*
Sickness	Mareo	*Mah-reh'-oh*
Insomnia	Insomnio	*In-saum'-ne-oh*
Sunburn	Quemadura del sol	*Keh-mah-doo'-rah dehl saul*
Insect bite	Picadura de insecto	*Pe-cah-doo'-rah deh in-sec'-toh*

AT THE DEPARTMENT STORES

Stairs	Escaleras	*Es-cah-leh'-rahs*
Escalator	Escaleras mecánicas	*Es-cah-leh'-rahs meh-cah'-ne-cahs*
Lift	Ascensor	*As-then-saur'*
Shelf	Estantería	*Es-tan-teh-ree'-ah*
Fitting room	Probador	*Prau-bah-daur'*
Sales	Rebajas	*Reh-bah'-hahs*
Ground floor	Planta baja	*Plahn'-tah bah'-hah*
First, second... floor	Primera, segunda... planta	*Pre-meh'-rah,seh-goon'-dah...* *plahn'-tah*
Record/gift/ underwear/toy/ sport... department	Sección de discos/ regalos/lencería/ juguetes/deportes...	*Sec-the-aun' deh dees'-cohs,* *reh-gah'-lohs, len-theh-ree'-ah,* *hoo-gheh'-tehs, deh-paur'-tehs ...*

CLOTHES AND ACCESSORIES

Overcoat	Abrigo	*Ah-bree'-goh*
Raincoat	Impermeable	*Im-per-meh-ah'-bleh*
Trench coat	Gabardina	*Gah-bar-dee'-nah*
Trousers	Pantalones	*Pan-tah-lau'-nehs*
Jeans	Vaqueros	*Vah-keh'-rohs*
Shorts	Pantalones	*Pan-tah-lau'-nehs caur'-tohs*
Pullover	Jersey	*Her-seh'-y*
Jacket	Chaqueta	*Chah-keh'-tah*

T-shirt	Camiseta	*Cah-me-seh'-tah*
Waistcoat	Chaleco	*Chah-leh'-coh*
Vest	Camiseta	*Cah-me-seh'-tah*
Underpants	Calzoncillos	*Cal-thaun-thee'-lyohs*
Socks	Calcetines	*Cal-theh-tee'-nes*
Tie	Corbata	*Caur-bah'-tah*
Shirt	Camisa	*Cah-mee'-sah*
Blouse	Blusa	*Bloo'-sah*
Skirt	Falda	*Fahl'-dah*
Cardigan	Rebeca	*Reh-beh'-cah*
Suit	Traje	*Trah'-heh*
Dress	Vestido	*Ves-tee'-doh*
Evening dress	Traje de noche	*Trah'-heh deh nau'-cheh*
Bra	Sujetador	*Soo-heh-tah-daur'*
Tights	Medias	*Meh'-de-ahs*
Knickers	Bragas	*Brah'-gahs*
Dressing gown	Bata	*Bah'-tah*
Pyjamas	Pijama	*Pe-hah'-mah*
Night gown	Camisón	*Cah-me-saun'*
Gloves	Guantes	*Goo-ahn'-tehs*
Scarf	Bufanda	*Boo-fahn'-dah*
Umbrella	Paraguas	*Pah-rah'-goo-ahs*
Handkerchief	Pañuelo	*Pah-nyoo-eh'-loh*
Belt	Cinturón	*Thin-too-raun'*
Handbag	Bolso	*Baul'-soh*
Purse	Monedero	*Mau-neh-deh'-roh*
Hat	Sombrero	*Saum-breh'-roh*
Fan	Abanico	*Ah-bah-nee'-coh*
Ring	Anillo	*Ah-nee'-lyoh*

Earring	Pendiente	*Pen-de-ehn'-teh*
Bracelet	Pulsera	*Pool-sch' rah*
Bathing costume	Bañador	*Bah-nyah-daur'*
Tracksuit	Chándal	*Chahn'-dal*
Sweat shirt	Sudadera	*Soo-dah-deh'-rah*

MATERIALS

Cotton	Algodón	*Al-gau-daun'*
Leather	Piel	*Pe-ehl'*
Linen	Lino	*Lee'-noh*
Wool	Lana	*Lah'-nah*
Velvet	Terciopelo	*Ter-the-au-peh'-loh*
Silk	Seda	*Seh'-dah*
Viscose	Viscosa	*Ves-cau'-sah*
Nylon	Nilón	*Ne-laun'*
Acrilic fibre	Acrílico	*Ah-cree'-le-coh*

COLOURS

White	Blanco	*Blahn'-coh*
Black	Negro	*Neh'-groh*
Red	Rojo	*Rau'-hoh*
Blue	Azul	*Ah-thool'*
Yellow	Amarillo	*Ah-mah-ree'-lyoh*
Brown	Marrón	*Mar-raun'*
Green	Verde	*Ver'-deh*
Grey	Gris	*Grees*
Beige	Beige	*Beish*
Purple	Morado	*Mau-rah'-doh*
Orange	Naranja	*Nah-rahn'-hah*
Pink	Rosa	*Rau'-sah*
Light	Claro	*Clah'-roh*
Dark	Oscuro	*Aus-coo'-roh*

In which floor is the leather goods department?	¿En qué planta está la sección de artículos de piel?
	En keh' plahn'-tah es-tah' lah sec-the-aun' deh ar-tee'-coo-lohs deh pe-ehl'?
On the ground floor	En la planta baja
	En lah plahn'-tah bah'-hah
I would like to see some striped shirts	Quisiera ver algunas camisas de rayas
	Ke-se-eh'-rah ver al-goo'-nahs cah-mee'-sahs deh rah'-yahs
I want it with short (long) sleeves	La quiero de manga corta (larga)
	Lah ke-eh'-roh deh mahn'-gah caur-tah (lar'-gah)
What material is it?	¿De qué es?
	Deh keh' es?
Have you got any other designs?	¿Tienen otros modelos?
	Te-eh'-nen au'-trohs mau-deh'-lohs?
What size, please?	¿De qué talla?
	Deh keh' tah'-lyah?
Is this my seize?	¿Me irá bien ésta?
	Meh e-rah' be-en' es'-tah?
Where is the fitting room?	¿Dónde está el probador?
	Daun'-deh es-tah' el prau-bah-daur'?
I'll try it on	Voy a probármela
	Vau'-y ah prau-bar'-meh-lah

Does it fit you?	¿Le queda bien?	*Leh keh'-dah be-en'?*
The collar is a little tight	El cuello me queda un poco apretado	*El coo-eh'-lyoh meh keh'-dah oon pau'-coh ah-preh-tah'-doh*
It has a wrinkle here	Me hace una arruga aquí	*Meh ah'-theh oo'-nah ar-roo'-gah ah-kee'*
I'll try a larger size	Voy a probarme una talla mayor	*Vau'-y ah prau-bar'-meh oo'-nah tah'-lyah mah-yaur'*
I'll take this one	Me quedo con ésta	*Meh keh'-doh caun es'-tah*
Please show me some natural silk ties	Por favor, enséñeme corbatas de seda natural	*Paur fah-vaur', en-seh'-nyeh-meh caur-bah'-tahs deh seh'-dah nah-too-rahl'*
In which colour?	¿De qué color?	*Deh keh' cau-laur'?*
Navy blue	Azul marino	*Ah-thool' mah-ree'-noh*
I like this one	Me gusta ésta	*Meh goos'-tah es'-tah*
How much is that all together?	¿Cuánto es todo?	*Coo-ahn'-toh es tau'-doh?*

Where is the cash?	¿Dónde está la caja?	
	Daun'-deh es-tah' lah cah'-hah?	

Will you pay cash or by credit card?	¿En efectivo o con tarjeta?	
	En eh-fec-tee'-voh au caun tar-heh'-tah?	

Could you gift-wrap it for me?	¿Podría envolvérmelo para regalo?	
	Pau-dree'-ah en-vaul-ver'-meh-loh pah'-rah reh-gah'-loh?	

AT THE SHOESHOP

Shoes	Zapatos	*Thah-pah'-tohs*
Boots	Botas	*Bau'-tahs*
Sandals	Sandalias	*San-dah'-le-ahs*
Moccasins	Mocasines	*Mau-cah-see'-nehs*
Slippers	Zapatillas	*Thah-pah-tee'-lyahs*
Sole	Suela	*Soo-eh'-lah*
Heel	Tacón	*Tah-caun'*
Shoelace	Cordón	*Caur-daun'*
Leather	Piel	*Pe-ehl'*
Suede	Ante	*Ahn'-teh*
Rubber	Goma	*Gau'-mah*

I want a pair of high-heeled shoes	Deseo un par de zapatos de tacón alto	
	Deh-seh'-oh oon par deh thah-pah'-tohs deh tah-caun' ahl'-toh	

| What kind do you want? | ¿Cómo los quiere? |
| | *Cau'-moh lohs ke-eh'-reh?* |

| With shoelaces and good for the rain | Con cordones y que sean buenos para la lluvia |
| | *Caun caur-dau'-nehs ee keh seh'-an boo-eh'-nohs pah'-rah lah lyoo'-ve-ah* |

| What size, please? | ¿Qué número calza? |
| | *Keh' noo'-meh-roh cahl'-thah?* |

| Will you please show me the pair in the window | Haga el favor de enseñarme los del escaparate |
| | *Ah'-gah el fah-vaur' deh en-seh-nyar'-meh lohs dehl es-cah-pah-rah'-teh* |

| They are a little tight | Me aprietan un poco |
| | *Meh ah-pre-eh'-tan oon pau'-coh* |

| They are too large | Me quedan demasiado grandes |
| | *Meh keh'-dan deh-mah-se-ah'-doh grahn'-dehs* |

| Try this size | Pruébese este otro número |
| | *Proo-eh'-beh-seh es'-teh au'-troh noo'-meh-roh* |

| This one fits well | Este me está bien |
| | *Es'-teh meh es-tah' be-en'* |

| How much are they? | ¿Cuánto valen? |
| | *Coo-ahn'-toh vah'-len?* |

AT THE PERFUMERY

Soap	Jabón	*Hah-baun'*
Shampoo	Champú	*Cham-poo'*
Deodorant	Desodorante	*Deh-sau-dau-rahn'-teh*
Shower gel	Gel de baño	*Hehl deh bah'-nyoh*
Hair spray	Laca	*Lah'-cah*
Sun tan cream	Bronceador	*Braun-theh-ah-daur'*
Comb	Peine	*Peh'-e-neh*
Hairbrush	Cepillo de dientes	*Theh-pee'-lyoh deh de-ehn'-tehs*
Toothbrush	Cepillo	*Theh-pee'-lyoh*
Toothpaste	Pasta de dientes	*Pas'-tah deh de-ehn'-tehs*
Make-up	Maquillaje	*Mah-ke-lyah'-heh*
Cologne water	Colonia	*Cau-lau'-ne-ah*
Nail varnish	Esmalte	*Es-mahl'-teh*
Mascara	Rímel	*Ree'-mel*
Lipstick	Barra de labios	*Bar'-rah deh lah'-be-ohs*
Perfume	Perfume	*Per-foo'-meh*
Scissors	Tijeras	*Te-heh'-rahs*
Razor	Maquinilla de afeitar	*Mah-ke-nee'-lyah deh ah-feh-e-tar'*
Lotion	Loción	*Lau-the-aun'*
Shaving foam	Espuma de afeitar	*Es-poo'-mah deh af-feh-e-tar'*
Cleansing cream	Crema limpiadora	*Creh'-mah lim-pe-ah-dau'-rah*
Face lotion	Loción facial	*Lau-the-aun' fah-the-ahl'*
Nourishing cream	Crema nutritiva	*Creh'-mah noo-tre-tee'-vah*
Hair remover	Depilatorio	*Deh-pe-lah-tau'-re-oh*

AT THE PHOTOGRAPHIC SHOP

Camera	Cámara	Cah'-mah-rah
Lens	Objetivo	Aub-heh-tee'-voh
View-finder	Visor	Ve-saur'
Filter	Filtro	Feel'-troh
Diaphragm	Diafragma	De-ah-frag'-mah
Trigger	Disparador	Dis-pah-rah-daur'
Camera film	Carrete	Car-reh'-teh
Colour	Color	Cau-laur'
Black and white	Blanco y negro	Blahn'-coh ee neh'-groh
Slide	Diapositiva	De-ah-pau-se-tee'-vah
Negative	Negativo	Neh-gah-tee'-voh
Size	Tamaño	Tah-mah'-nyoh
Enlargement	Ampliación	Am-ple-ah-the-aun'
Print (copy)	Copia	Cau'-pe-ah
Photograph	Foto	Fau'-toh
Battery	Pila	Pee'-lah
Gloss	Brillo	Bree'-lyoh
Matt	Mate	Mah'-teh

Would you give me a 24 exposure film for this camera?		Por favor, ¿me da un carrete de 24 fotos para esta cámara?
		Paur fah-vaur', meh dah oon car-reh'-teh deh veh'-in-te-coo-ah'-troh fau'-tohs pah'-rah es'-tah cah'-mah-rah?

| How much does the developing cost? | ✎ | ¿Cuánto cuesta el revelado? |
| | 💬 | *Coo-ahn'-toh coo-es'-tah el reh-veh-lah'-doh?* |

| Could you develop this film with two prints of each photograph? | ✎ | ¿Puede revelar este carrete y sacar dos copias de cada foto? |
| | 💬 | *Poo-eh'-deh reh-veh-lar' es'-teh car-reh'-teh ee sah-car' daus cau'-pe-ahs deh cah'-dah fau'-toh?* |

| Can you enlarge these prints? | ✎ | ¿Puede ampliarme estas copias? |
| | 💬 | *Poo-eh'-deh am-ple-ar'-meh es'-tahs cau'-pe-ahs?* |

| Do you take passport photographs? | ✎ | ¿Hace usted fotos de carné? |
| | 💬 | *Ah'-theh oos-ted' fau'-tohs deh car-neh'?* |

| My camera won't work, can you see what is wrong with it? | ✎ | Mi cámara no funciona, ¿puede Vd. ver qué le pasa? |
| | 💬 | *Mee cah'-mah-rah noh foon-the-au'-nah, poo-eh'-deh oos-ted' ver keh' leh pah'-sah?* |

AT THE OPTICIAN'S

Glasses	Gafas	*Gah'-fahs*
Contact lenses	Lentes de contacto (lentillas)	*Lehn'-tehs deh caun-tac'-toh (len-tee'-lyahs)*
Sun glasses	Gafas de sol	*Gah'-fahs deh saul*
Lens	Cristal	*Cris-tahl'*
Frame	Montura	*Maun-too'-rah*

I have broken the frames of my glasses. Can you repair them?

Se me ha roto la montura de las gafas. ¿Pueden arreglármela?

Seh meh ah rau'-toh lah maun-too'-rah deh lahs gah'-fahs. Poo-eh'-den ar-reh-glar'-meh-lah?

When will they be ready?

¿Cuándo estarán listas?

Coo-ahn'-doh es-tah-rahn' lees'-tahs?

I have broken a lens. Can you replace it?

Se me ha roto un cristal. ¿Pueden hacerme otro nuevo?

Seh meh ah rau'-toh oon cris-tahl'. Poo-eh'-den ah-thehr'-meh au'-troh noo-eh'-voh?

I am looking for some cleaning fluid for contact lenses

Necesito un líquido limpiador de lentillas

Neh-theh-see'-toh oon lee'-ke-doh lim-pe-ah-daur' deh len-tee'-lyahs

---

I would like to have my eyes tested

Quiero graduarme la vista

Ke-eh'-roh grah-doo-ar'-meh lah vees'-tah

AT THE FLORIST'S

Rose	Rosa	*Rau'-sah*
Carnation	Clavel	*Clah-vehl'*
Daisy	Margarita	*Mar-gah-ree'-tah*
Orchid	Orquídea	*Aur-kee'-deh-ah*
Iris	Lirio	*Lee'-re-oh*
White lily	Azucena	*Ah-thoo-theh'-nah*
Violet	Violeta	*Ve-au-leh'-tah*
Pansy	Pensamiento	*Pen-sah-me-ehn'-toh*
Dahlia	Dalia	*Dah'-le-ah*
Spikenard	Nardo	*Nar'-doh*
Gardenia	Gardenia	*Gar-deh'-ne-ah*
Hyacinth	Jacinto	*Hah-thin'-toh*
Daffodil	Narciso	*Nar-thee'-soh*
Chrysanthemum	Crisantemo	*Cri-san-teh'-moh*
Tulip	Tulipán	*Too-le-pahn'*

I would like to order a bouquet	✏️ Quería encargar un ramo de flores
	💬 *Keh-ree'-ah en-car-gar' oon rah'-moh deh flau'-rehs*

You can choose roses or carnations in several colours	✏️ Puede escoger entre rosas o claveles de varios colores
	💬 *Poo-eh'-deh es-cau-her' ehn'-treh rau'-sas au clah-veh'-lehs deh vah'-re-ohs cau-lau'-rehs*

| I want a dried flower arrangement | Deseo un centro de flores secas |
| | *Deh-seh'-oh oon thehn'-troh deh flau'-rehs seh'-cahs* |

| What are these flowers called? | ¿Cómo se llaman estas flores? |
| | *Cau'-moh seh lyah'-man es'-tahs flau'-rehs?* |

| How much is this fern? | ¿Cuánto cuesta este helecho? |
| | *Coo-anh'-toh coo-es'-tah es'-teh eh-leh'-choh?* |

| Can you send it to this address before twelve tomorrow? | ¿Pueden mandarlo a esta dirección mañana antes de las doce? |
| | *Poo-eh'-den man-dar'-loh ah es'-tah de-rec-the-aun' mah-nyah'-nah ahn'-tes deh lahs dau'-theh?* |

| Could you please send also this card? | Envíen también esta tarjeta, por favor |
| | *En-ve'-en tam-be-ehn' es'-tah tar-heh'-tah, paur fah-vaur'* |

AT THE TOBACCONIST'S

Tobacco	Tabaco	*Tah-bah'-coh*
Tobacconist's	Estanco	*Es-tahn'-coh*
Cigarette	Cigarrillo	*The-gar-ree'-lyoh*
Virginian/black	Rubio/negro	*Roo'-be-oh/neh'-groh*
Cigar	Puro	*Poo'-roh*
Matches	Cerillas	*Theh-ree'-lyahs*
Lighter	Encendedor (mechero)	*En-then-deh-daur (meh-cheh'-roh)*
Pipe	Pipa	*Pee'-pah*
Cigarette holder	Boquilla	*Bau-kee'-lyah*
Stamp	Sello	*Seh'-lyoh*
Envelope	Sobre	*Sau'-breh*
Bus pass	Bonobús	*Bau'-noh-boos*

Give me a packet of filter tipped cigarettes	✎ Deme un paquete de cigarrillos con filtro
	💬 *Deh'-meh oon pah-keh'-teh deh the-gar-ree'-lyohs caun feel'-troh*

Give me a box of matches too	✎ Deme también una caja de cerillas
	💬 *Deh'-meh tam-be-ehn' oo'-nah cah'-hah deh theh-ree'-lyahs*

I want two stamps for ..., a bus pass and a postcard	✎ Quiero dos sellos para ..., un bonobús y una postal
	💬 *Ke-eh'-roh daus seh'-lyohs, oon bau-noh-boos' ee oo'-nah paus-tahl'*

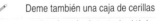

AT THE HAIRDRESSER'S

Hairdresser	Peluquero/a	Peh-loo-keh'-roh/rah
Hair	Pelo (cabello)	Peh'-loh (cah-beh'-lyoh)
Scissors	Tijeras	Te-heh'-rahs
Comb	Peine	Peh'-e-neh
Brush	Cepillo	Theh-pee'-lyoh
Dryer	Secador	Seh-cah-daur'
Hair cut	Corte de pelo	Caur'-teh deh peh'-loh
Shampooing	Lavado	Lah-vah'-doh
Hair style	Peinado	Peh-e-nah'-doh
Manicure	Manicura	Mah-ne-coo'-rah
Dyeing	Tinte	Tin'-teh
Shave	Afeitado	Ah-feh-e-tah'-doh
Beard	Barba	Bar'-bah
Moustache	Bigote	Be-gau'-teh
Sideboards	Patillas	Pah-tee'-lyahs
Fringe	Flequillo	Fleh-kee'-lyoh
Curl	Rizo	Ree'-thoh
Plait	Trenza	Trehn'-thah

I want a shave	Deseo afeitarme
	Deh-seh'-oh ah-feh-e-tar'-meh

A razor cut, please	Córteme el pelo a navaja
	Caur'-teh-meh el peh'-loh ah nah-vah'-hah

Just a trim	No me corte mucho
	Noh meh caur'-teh moo'-choh

| Trim the moustache | Arrégleme el bigote |
| | *Ar-reh'-gleh-meh el be-gau'-teh* |

| A shampoo, please | Lávemelo, por favor |
| | *Lah'-veh-meh-loh, paur fah-vaur'* |

| I have dandruff | Tengo caspa |
| | *Tehn'-goh cas'-pah* |

| The water is too hot/cold | El agua está demasiado caliente/fría |
| | *El ah'-goo-ah es-tah' deh-mah-se-ah'-doh cah-le-ehn'-teh/free'-ah* |

| I would like to have my hair washed and set | Lavar y peinar |
| | *Lah-var' ee peh-e-nar'* |

| How long shall I have to wait? | ¿Cuánto tendré que esperar? |
| | *Coo-ahn'-toh ten-dreh' keh es-peh-rar'?* |

| My hair is greasy/dry | Tengo el cabello graso/seco |
| | *Tehn'-goh el cah-beh'-lyoh grah'-soh/seh'-coh* |

| I am losing a lot of hair | Se me cae mucho el pelo |
| | *Seh meh cah'-eh moo'-choh el peh'-loh* |

| Trim the ends | ¡Córteme sólo las puntas! |
| | *Caur'-teh-meh sau'-loh lahs poon'-tahs!* |

| I would like a hair cut like this | Quiero un corte como éste |
| | *Ke-eh'-roh oon caur'-teh cau'-moh es'-teh* |

| I would like to dye my hair/have a permanent wave | Quisiera teñirme el pelo/ hacerme una permanente |
| | *Ke-se-eh'-rah teh-nyeer'-meh el peh'-loh/ ah-thehr'-meh oo'-nah per-mah-nehn'-teh* |

| Same colour? | ¿Del mismo color? |
| | *Dehl mees'-moh cau-laur'?* |

| A little darker/lighter | Un poco más oscuro/más claro |
| | *Oon pau'-coh mas aus-coo'-roh/mas clah'-roh* |

| How shall I set your hair? | ¿Cómo la peino? |
| | *Cau'-moh lah peh'-e-noh?* |

| Towards the back, without any parting | Todo hacia atrás, sin raya |
| | *Tau'-doh ah'-the-ah ah-tras', sin rah'-yah* |

| However you want | Como le parezca |
| | *Cau'-moh leh pah-reth'-cah* |

| That's fine, thank you | Así está bien, gracias |
| | *Ah-see' es-tah' be-en', grah'-the-ahs* |

LEISURE

MUSEUMS AND PLACES OF INTEREST

Museum	Museo	*Moo-seh'-oh*
Cathedral	Catedral	*Cah-teh-drahl'*
Monument	Monumento	*Mau-noo-mehn'-toh*
Visiting hours	Horas de visita	*Au'-rahs deh ve-see'-tah*
Free entry	Entrada libre	*En-trah'-dah*
Ticket	Entrada	*En-trah'-dah lee'-breh*
Open	Abierto	*Ah-be-er'-toh*
Closed	Cerrado	*Ther-rah'-doh*
Brochure	Catálogo	*Cah-tah'-lau-goh*
Guide	Guía	*Ghee'-ah*
Halls	Salas	*Sah'-lahs*
Exhibition	Exposición	*Ex-pau-se-the-aun'*
Picture	Cuadro (pintura)	*Coo-ah'-droh (pin-too'-rah)*
Drawing	Dibujo	*De-boo'-hoh*
Engraving	Grabado	*Grah-bah'-doh*
Sculpture	Escultura	*Es-cool-too'-rah*
Art	Arte	*Ar'-teh*
Chapel	Capilla	*Cah-pee'-lyah*
Cloister	Claustro	*Clah'-oos-troh*
Dome	Cúpula	*Coo'-poo-lah*
Nave	Nave	*Nah'-veh*
Palace	Palacio	*Pah-lah'-the-oh*
Tower	Torre	*Taur'-reh*
Courtyard	Patio	*Pah'-te-oh*
Marble	Mármol	*Mar'-maul*
Bronze	Bronce	*Braun'-theh*
Stone	Piedra	*Pe-eh'-drah*

What places of interest are there in the town?

¿Qué lugares de interés hay en la ciudad?

Keh' loo-gah'-rehs deh in-teh-rehs' ah'-y en lah the-oo-dad'?

The ... Museum, St... Church and the Town Hall are specially interesting for tourists

El museo..., la iglesia de San... y el Ayuntamiento tienen un especial interés turístico

El moo-seh'-oh..., lah e-gleh'-se-ah deh sahn... ee el ah-yoon-tah-me-ehn'-toh te-eh'-nen oon es-peh-the-ahl' in-teh-rehs' too-rees'-te-coh

---

What time does the Fine Arts Museum open/close?

¿A qué hora abre/cierra el Museo de Bellas Artes?

Ah keh' au'-rah ah'-breh/the-er'-rah el moo-seh'-oh deh beh'-lyahs ar'-tehs?

Is it possible to have a guided tour?

¿Se puede hacer una visita con guía?

Seh poo-eh'-deh ah'-thehr oo'-nah ve-see'-tah caun ghee'-ah?

Pictures forbidden

Prohibido hacer fotografías

Prau-e-bee'-doh ah-thehr' fau-tau-grah-fee'-ahs

Which century is it from?

¿De qué siglo es?

Deh keh' see'-gloh es?

Is it possible to go up the bell tower?

¿Se puede subir al campanario?

Seh poo-eh'-deh soo-beer' ahl cam-pah-nah'-re-oh?

ENTERTAINMENT

Concert hall	Sala de conciertos	*Sah'-lah deh caun-the-er'-tohs*
Theatre	Teatro	*Teh-ah'-troh*
Cinema	Cine	*Thee'-neh*
Ticket	Entrada	*En-trah'-dah*
Booking office	Taquilla	*Tah-kee'-lyah*
List of plays	Cartelera	*Car-teh-leh'-rah*
Seat	Asiento	*Ah-se-ehn'-toh*
Row	Fila	*Fee'-lah*
Aisle	Pasillo	*Pah-see'-lyoh*
Cloakroom	Guardarropa	*Goo-ar-dah-rau'-pah*
Usher	Acomodador	*Ah-cau-mau-dah-daur'*
Première	Estreno	*Es-treh'-noh*

CONCERTS

Music	Música	*Moo'-se-cah*
Musician	Músico	*Moo'-se-coh*
Orchestra	Orquesta	*Aur-kes'-tah*
Conductor	Director	*De-rec-taur'*
Singer	Cantante	*Can-tahn'-teh*
Audience	Público	*Poo'-ble-coh*

Which orchestra is playing?		¿Qué orquesta toca?
		Keh' aur-kes'-tah tau'-cah?

131

| Give me two boxes for this evening's concert | ✏️ | Deme dos palcos para el concierto de esta noche |
| | 💬 | *Deh'-meh daus pahl'-cohs pah'-rah el caun-the-er'-toh deh es'-tah nau'-cheh* |

| I would like a seat in the front row | ✏️ | Deseo un asiento en la primera fila |
| | 💬 | *Deh-seh'-oh oon ah-se-ehn'-toh en lah pre-meh'-rah fee'-lah* |

THEATRE

Play	Obra	*Au'-brah*
Actor	Actor	*Ac-taur'*
Actress	Actriz	*Ac-treeth'*
Stage	Escenario	*Es-theh-nah'-re-oh*
Curtain	Telón	*Teh-laun'*
Scenery	Decorados	*Deh-cau-rah'-dohs*
Show	Función	*Foon-the-aun'*
Act	Acto	*Ac'-toh*
Interval	Entreacto	*En-treh-ac'-toh*

| What is on at the ... Theatre tonight? | ✏️ | ¿Qué ponen en el Teatro ... esta noche? |
| | 💬 | *Keh' pau'-nen en el teh-ah'-troh ... es'-tah nau'-cheh?* |

| Which theatre is the ballet by ... on at? | ✏️ | ¿En qué teatro ponen el ballet de ...? |
| | 💬 | *En keh' teh-ah'-troh pau'-nen el bah-leht' deh ...?* |

| How long does the play last? | ✏️ | ¿Cuánto dura la obra? |
| | 💬 | *Coo-ahn'-toh doo'-rah lah au'-brah?* |

| Two stalls in the centre, please | ✏️ | Dos butacas centrales, por favor |
| | 💬 | *Daus boo-tah'-cahs then-trah'-lehs, paur fah-vaur'* |

CINEMA

Film	Película	*Peh-lee'-coo-lah*
Screen	Pantalla	*Pan-tah'-lyah*
Film-show	Sesión	*Seh-se-aun'*
Documentary	Documental	*Dau-coo-men-tahl'*
Cartoons	Dibujos animados	*De-boo'-hohs ah-ne-mah'-dohs*

Where is the new film by ... on?	✏	¿Dónde se proyecta la nueva película de ...?
	💬	*Daun'-deh seh prau-yec'-tah lah noo-eh'-vah peh-lee'-coo-lah deh ...?*

Is it in the original language with subtitles?	✏	¿Es en versión original con subtítulos?
	💬	*Es en ver'-se-aun' au-re-ge-nahl' caun soob-tee'-too-lohs?*

No, it is dubbed	✏	No, está doblada
	💬	*Noh, es-tah' dau-blah'-dah*

ON THE BEACH/ AT THE SWIMMING POOL

Beach	Playa	*Plah'-yah*
Sea	Mar	*Mar*
Swimming pool	Piscina	*Pis-thee'-nah*
Sand	Arena	*Ah-reh'-nah*
Wave	Ola	*Au'-lah*
Shore	Orilla	*Au-ree'-lyah*
Boat	Barca	*Bar'-cah*

Sunshade	Sombrilla	*Saum-bree'-lyah*
Sun bed	Tumbona	*Toom-bau'-nah*
Bathing costume	Bañador	*Bah-nyah-daur'*
Spring board	Trampolín	*Tram-pau-leen'*
Shower	Ducha	*Doo'-chah*

| Is it dangerous to swim here? | ✏️ ¿Es peligroso bañarse aquí? |
| | 💬 *Es peh-lee-grau'-soh bah-nyar'-seh ah-kee'?* |

| The water is dirty (polluted) | ✏️ El agua está sucia (contaminada) |
| | 💬 *El ah'-goo-ah es-tah' soo'-the-ah (caun-tah-me-nah'-dah)* |

| Are there lifeguards? | ✏️ ¿Hay socorristas? |
| | 💬 *Ah'-y sau-caur-rees'-tahs?* |

CAMPING

Camp-site	Camping	*Cahm'-pin*
Tent	Tienda de campaña	*Te-en'-dah deh cam-pah'-nyah*
Caravan	Caravana	*Cah-rah-vah'-nah*
Sleeping bag	Saco de dormir	*Sah'-coh deh daur-meer'*
Hammer	Martillo	*Mar-tee'-lyoh*
Lamp	Linterna	*Lin-ter'-nah*
Butane cylinder	Bombona de butano	*Baum-bau'-nah deh boo-tah'-noh*
Tin-opener	Abrelatas	*Ah-breh-lah'- tahs*
Pocket knife	Navaja	*Nah-vah'-hah*
Corkscrew	Sacacorchos	*Sah-cah-caur'-chohs*
Electric point	Enchufe	*En-choo'-feh*
Toilets	Servicios	*Ser-vee'-the-ohs*

I am looking for a camp-site near the beach	✏️	Estoy buscando un camping cerca de la playa
	💬	*Es-tau'-y boos-cahn'-doh oon cahm'-pin thehr'-cah deh lah plah'-yah*

Can you tell me the daily fee?	✏️	¿Cuál es la tarifa diaria?
	💬	*Coo-ahl' es lah tah-ree'-fah de-ah'-re-ah?*

Can we pitch the tent here?	✏️	¿Podemos montar la tienda aquí?
	💬	*Pau-deh'-mohs maun-tar' lah te-ehn'-dah ah-kee'?*

Where can I park my car?	✏️	¿Dónde puedo aparcar el coche?
	💬	*Daun'-deh poo-eh'-doh ah-par-car' el cau'-cheh?*

I would like to stay for ... days	✏️	Quiero quedarme ... días
	💬	*Ke-eh'-roh keh-dar'-meh ... dee'-ahs*

Is the water drinkable?	✏️	¿Es agua potable?
	💬	*Es ah'-goo-ah pau-tah'-bleh?*

Can we light a fire?	✏️	¿Podemos encender fuego?
	💬	*Pau-deh'-mohs en-thehn-der' foo-eh'-goh?*

Is there a night watchman on the camp-site?	✏️	¿Hay vigilancia nocturna?
	💬	*Ah'-y ve-he-lahn'-the-ah nauc-toor'-nah?*

Is there a supermarket near?	✏️	¿Hay un supermercado cerca?
	💬	*Ah'-y oon soo-per-mer-cah'-doh thehr'-cah?*

SPORTS

Sports centre	Polideportivo	*Pau-le-deh-paur-tee'-voh*
Tennis court	Pista de tenis	*Pees'-tah deh teh'-nihs*
Gym	Gimnasio	*Him-nah'-se-oh*
Golf course	Campo de golf	*Cahm'-poh deh gaulf*
Football ground	Campo de fútbol	*Cahm'-poh deh foot'-baul*
Swimming pool	Piscina	*Pis-thee'-nah*

Where is the nearest ...?
¿Dónde está el/la ... más próximo/a?
Daun'-deh es-tah' el/lah ... mas prauc'-se-moh/ah?

I would like to hire a sailboard
Quería alquilar una tabla de windsurfing
Keh-ree'-ah al-ke-lar' oo'-nah tah'-blah deh windsurfing

Is there a water-skiing instructor?
¿Hay monitores de esquí acuático?
Ah'-y mau-ne-tau'-rehs deh es-kee' ah-coo-ah'-te-coh?

Can I have a lesson?
¿Puedo tener una clase?
Poo-eh'-doh teh-ner' oo'-nah clah'-seh?

How much does a one-hour lesson cost?
¿Cuánto cuesta una hora de clase?
Coo-ahn'-toh coo-es'-tah oo'-nah au'-rah deh clah'-seh?

I would like to book the court for tomorrow at ...
Quisiera reservar la pista para mañana a las ...
Ke-se-eh'-rah reh-ser-var' lah pees'-tah pah'-rah mah-nyah'-nah ah lahs ...

USEFUL SERVICES

BANK

Bank	Banco	*Bahn'-coh*
Savings bank	Caja de ahorros	*Cah'-hah deh ah-aur'-rohs*
Exchange	Cambio	*Cahm'-be-oh*
Money	Dinero	*De-neh'-roh*
Coin	Moneda	*Mau-neh'-dah*
Note	Billete	*Be-lyeh'-teh*
Cheque	Cheque	*Cheh'-keh*
Counter	Ventanilla	*Ven-tah-nee'-lyah*
Receipt	Recibo	*Reh-thee'-boh*
Interest	Interés	*In-teh-res'*
Credit card	Tarjeta de crédito	*Tar-heh'-tah deh creh'-de-toh*
Traveller's cheque	Cheque de viaje	*Cheh'-keh deh ve-ah'-heh*
Exchange rate	Cotización	*Cau-te-thah-the-aun'*
Foreign currency	Divisas	*De-vee'-sahs*
Cashdesk	Caja	*Cah'-hah*
Cash dispenser	Cajero automático	*Cah-heh'-roh ah-oo-tau-mah'-te-coh*
Current account	Cuenta corriente	*Coo-ehn'-tah caur-re-en'-teh*
Bill of exchange	Letra de cambio	*Leh'-trah deh cahm'-be-oh*

Where can I change my money?	¿Dónde puedo cambiar dinero?
	Daun'-deh poo-eh'-doh cam-be-ar' de-neh'-roh?

What are the banking hours?	¿Cúal es el horario de los bancos?
	Coo-ahl' es el au-rah'-re-oh deh lohs bahn'-cohs?

I would like to change this traveller's cheque	✎	Quería cambiar este cheque de viaje
	💬	*Keh-ree'-ah cam-be-ar' es'-teh cheh'-keh deh ve-ah'-heh*

Have you received a transfer from ... addressed to ...?	✎	¿Han recibido una transferencia de ... a nombre de ...?
	💬	*Ahn reh-the-bee'-doh oo'-nah trans-feh-rehn'-the-ah deh ... ah nuum'-breh deh ...*

Can I cash this bearer cheque?	✎	¿Puedo cobrar este cheque al portador?
	💬	*Poo-eh'-doh cau-brar' es'-teh cheh'-keh ahl paur-tah-daur'?*

Sign here, please	✎	Firme aquí, por favor
	💬	*Feer'-meh ah-kee', paur fah-vaur'*

Go to the cashdesk (counter number...)	✎	Pase por caja (ventanilla número...)
	💬	*Pah'-seh paur cah'-hah (ven-tah-nee'-lyah noo'-meh-roh...)*

POST OFFICE

Post office	Correos	*Caur-reh'-ohs*
Letter	Carta	*Car'-tah*
Postcard	Postal	*Paus-tahl'*
Stamp	Sello	*Seh'-lyoh*
Postage	Franqueo	*Fran-keh'-oh*
Parcel	Paquete	*Pah-keh'-teh*
Poste restante	Lista de correos	*Lees'-tah deh caur-reh'-ohs*
Address	Dirección	*De-rec-the-aun'*
Postal code	Código postal	*Cau'-de-goh paus-tahl'*
Sender	Remitente	*Reh-me-tehn'-teh*
Addressee	Destinatario	*Des-te-nah-tah'-re-oh*
By post	Por correo	*Paur caur-reh'-oh*
Air mail	Por avión	*Paur ah-ve-aun'*
Registered letter	Carta certificada	*Car'-tah ther-te-fe-cah'-dah*
Express letter	Carta urgente	*Car'-tah oor-hehn'-teh*
Printed matter	Impresos	*Im-preh'-sohs*
Cash on delivery	Contra reembolso	*Caun'-trah reh-em-baul'-soh*
P.O. Box	Apartado de correos	*Ah-par-tah'-doh deh caur-reh'-ohs*

What time is the post office open?	¿A qué hora abre Correos?
	Ah keh' au'-rah ah'-breh caur-reh'-os?

You also can buy stamps in the tobacconist's	También puede comprar sellos en los estancos
	Tam-be-ehn' poo-eh'-deh caum-prar' seh'-lyohs en lohs es-tahn'-cohs

What is the postage for a postcard to England?	¿Cuál es el franqueo de una postal para Inglaterra?	*Coo-ahl' es el frahn-keh'-oh deh oo'-nah paus-tahl' pah'-rah In-glah-ter'-rah?*
Which is the counter for registered mail?	¿Cuál es la ventanilla de Certificados?	*Coo-ahl' es lah ven-tah-nee'-lyah deh ther-te-fe-cah'-dohs?*
I want to send this parcel by air mail	Quiero enviar este paquete por avión	*Ke-eh'-roh en-ve-ar' es'-teh pah-keh'-teh paur ah-ve-aun'*
Are there any letters poste restante in the name of ...?	¿Hay cartas a nombre de ... en Lista de Correos?	*Ah'-y car'-tahs ah naum'-breh deh ... en lees'-tah deh caur-reh'-ohs?*
What documents do I need to collect a package?	¿Qué documentos necesito para recoger un paquete?	*Keh' dau-coo-mehn'-tohs ne-theh-see'-toh pah'-rah reh-cau-her' oon pah-keh'-teh?*
Can you help me to fill in this form?	¿Puede ayudarme a rellenar este impreso?	*Poo-eh'-deh ah-yoo-dar'-meh ah reh-lyeh-nar' es'-teh im-preh'-soh?*
I would like to cash this postal order	Deseo cobrar este giro postal	*Deh-seh'-oh cau-brar' es'-teh hee'-roh paus-tahl'*
How much does a telegram to ... cost?	¿Cuánto cuesta un telegrama a ...?	*Coo-ahn'-toh coo-es'-tah oon teh-leh-grah'-mah ah ...?*

TELEPHONE

Public telephone	Teléfono público	*Teh-leh'-fau-noh poo'-ble-coh*
Phone box	Cabina	*Cah-bee'-nah*
Number	Número	*Noo'-meh-roh*
Code	Prefijo	*Preh-fee'-hoh*
Telephone call	Llamada	*Lyah-mah'-dah*
Coins	Monedas	*Mau-neh'-dahs*

I would like to make a collect call to ...
Quiero hacer una llamada a cobro revertido a ...
Ke-eh'-roh ah-thehr' oo'-nah lyah-mah'-dah ah cau'-broh reh-ver-tee'-doh ah ...

What is the code number for ...?
¿Cuál es el prefijo de ...?
Coo-ahl' es el preh-fee'-hoh deh ...?

What is the phone number for inquiries?
¿Cuál es el número de Información?
Coo-ahl' es el noo'-meh-roh deh in-faur-ma-the-aun'?

There is no answer
No contestan
Noh caun-tehs'-tan

It is engaged
Está comunicando
Es-tah' cau-moo-ne-cahn'-doh

You have got the wrong number
Se ha equivocado
Seh ah eh-ke-vau-cah'-doh

| Hello! | ¡Dígame! |
| | *Dee'-gah-meh!* |

| This is ... | Soy ... |
| | *Sau'-y ...* |

| May I speak to ...? | ¿Puedo hablar con ...? |
| | *Poo-eh'-doh ah-blar' caun...?* |

| It is me | Soy yo |
| | *Sau'-y yoh* |

| Just a moment, please | Un momento, por favor |
| | *Oon mau-mehn'-toh, paur fah-vaur'* |

| Who is calling? | ¿De parte de quién? |
| | *Deh par'-teh deh ke-ehn'?* |

| Hold the line | No cuelgue |
| | *Noh coo-ehl'-gheh* |

| He is out | Ha salido |
| | *Ah sah-lee'-doh* |

| Would you like to leave a message? | ¿Quiere dejarle un recado? |
| | *Ke-eh'-reh deh-har'-leh oon reh-cah'-doh?* |

| Tell him/her that ... has called | Dígale que ... ha llamado |
| | *Dee'-gah-leh keh ... ah lyah-mah'-doh* |

HEALTH

THE HUMAN BODY

Head	Cabeza	*Cah-beh'-thah*
Face	Cara	*Cah'-rah*
Eye	Ojo	*Au'-hoh*
Nose	Nariz	*Nah-reeth'*
Ear	Oído (oreja)	*Au-ee'-doh (au-reh'-hah)*
Mouth	Boca	*Bau'-cah*
Tongue	Lengua	*Lehn'-goo-ah*
Throat	Garganta	*Gar-gahn'-tah*
Neck	Cuello	*Coo-eh'-lyoh*
Shoulder	Hombro	*Aum'-broh*
Arm	Brazo	*Brah'-thoh*
Elbow	Codo	*Cau'-doh*
Wrist	Muñeca	*Moo-nyeh'-cah*
Hand	Mano	*Mah'-noh*
Finger	Dedo	*Deh'-doh*
Back	Espalda	*Es-pahl'-dah*
Chest	Pecho	*Peh'-choh*
Leg	Pierna	*Pe-er'-nah*
Knee	Rodilla	*Rau-dee'-lyah*
Foot	Pie	*Pe-eh'*
Toe	Dedo del pie	*Deh'-doh dehl pe-eh'*
Heart	Corazón	*Cau-rah-thaun'*
Stomach	Estómago	*Es-tau'-mah-goh*
Lung	Pulmón	*Pool-maun'*
Liver	Hígado	*Ee'-gah-doh*
Kidneys	Riñones	*Re-nyau'-nehs*
Intestines	Intestinos	*In-tes-tee'-nohs*

AT THE DOCTOR'S

Doctor	Médico	*Meh'-de-coh*
Nurse	Enfermera	*En-fer-meh'-rah*
Patient	Paciente	*Pah-thie-ehn'-teh*
Illness	Enfermedad	*En-fer-meh-dad'*
Pain	Dolor	*Dau-laur'*
Surgery (room)	Consulta	*Caun-sool'-tah*
Waiting room	Sala de espera	*Sah'-lah deh es-peh'-rah*
X-ray	Rayos X	*Rah'-yohs eh'-kis*
Prescription	Receta	*Reh-theh'-tah*
Blood pressure	Presión sanguínea	*Preh-se-aun' san-ghee'-neh-ah*
Blood group	Grupo sanguíneo	*Groo'-poh san-ghee'-neh-oh*

Can you call a doctor?	¿Puede llamar a un médico?
	Poo-eh'-deh lyah-mar' ah oon meh'-de-coh?

Do you know a doctor who speaks English?	¿Conoce a algún médico que hable inglés?
	Cau-nau'-theh ah al-goon' meh'-de-coh keh ah'-bleh in-gles'?

Can you take me to the Casualty Department?	¿Puede llevarme a Urgencias?
	Poo-eh'-deh lyeh-var'-meh ah Oor-hehn'-the-ahs?

I don't feel well	No me siento bien
	Noh meh se-ehn'-toh be-en'

What is the matter?	¿Qué le pasa?
	Keh' leh pah'-sah?

| I have got ... | Tengo ...
Tehn'-goh ... |

flu	gripe	*gree'-peh*
a headache	dolor de cabeza	*dau-laur' deh cah-beh'-thah*
a stomach ache	dolor de estómago	*dau-laur' deh es-tau'-mah-goh*
a sore throat	dolor de garganta	*dau-laur' deh gar-gahn'-tah*
a cough	tos	*taus*
a temperature	fiebre	*fe-eh'-breh*

| I have got a cold | Estoy resfriado/a
Es-tau'-y res-fre-ah'-doh/-dah |

| I am suffering
from dizzy spells | Tengo mareos
Tehn'-goh mah-reh'-ohs |

| I think I have broken
my leg | Creo que me he roto una pierna
Creh'-oh keh meh eh rau'-toh oo'-nah pe-er'-nah |

| I have sprained my ankle | Me he torcido un tobillo
Meh eh taur-thee'-doh oon tau-bee'-lyoh |

| I have difficulties
in breathing | Me cuesta trabajo respirar
Meh coo-es'-tah trah-bah'-hoh res-pe-rar' |

| Where does it hurt? | ¿Dónde le duele?
Daun'-deh leh doo-eh'-leh? |

| How long have
you been ill? | ¿Desde cuándo está enfermo?
Des'-deh coo-ahn'-doh es-tah' en-fer'-moh? |

| I am allergic to ... | Soy alérgico a ... |
| | *Sau'-y ah-ler'-he-coh ah ...* |

| I am in my ... week of pregnancy | Estoy embarazada de ... semanas |
| | *Es-tau'-y em-bah-rah-thah'-dah deh ... seh-mah'-nahs* |

| Breath, cough, put out your tongue | Respire, tosa, saque la lengua |
| | *Res-pee'-reh, tau'-sah, sah'-keh lah lehn'-goo-ah* |

| Undress, please | Quítese la ropa, por favor |
| | *Kee'-teh-seh lah rau'-pah, paur fah-vaur'* |

| You must stay in bed for ... days | Debe quedarse en cama ... días |
| | *Deh'-beh keh-dar'-seh en cah'-mah ... dee'-ahs* |

| Take these pills every ... hours | Tome estas pastillas cada ... horas |
| | *Tau'-meh es'-tahs pas-tee'-lyahs cah'-dah ... au'-rahs* |

DENTIST

Teeth	Dientes	*De-ehn'-tehs*
Back tooth	Muela	*Moo-eh'-lah*
Wisdom tooth	Muela del juicio	*Moo-eh'-lah dehl hoo-ee'-the-oh*
Gum	Encía	*En-thee'-ah*
Tooth decay	Caries	*Cah'-re-es*
Filling	Empaste	*Em-pas'-teh*

| This tooth hurts | Me duele este diente (muela) |
| | *Meh doo-eh'-leh es'-teh de-ehn'-teh (moo-eh'-lah)* |

| I must take it out | Habrá que sacarla |
| | *Ah-brah' keh sah-car'-lah* |

Give me a sedative	✎ Deme un calmante
	💬 *Deh'-meh oon cal-mahn'-teh*

The filling has fallen out	✎ Se me ha caído el empaste
	💬 *Seh meh ah cah-ee'-doh el em-pas'-teh*

Can you fill it at once?	✎ ¿Puede empastármelo en seguida?
	💬 *Poo-eh'-deh em-pas-tar'-meh-loh en seh-ghee'-dah?*

POLICE STATION

Police station	Comisaría	*Cau-me-sah-ree'-ah*
Police	Policía	*Pau-le-thee'-ah*
Police officer	Policía	*Pau-le-thee'-ah*
Report	Denuncia	*Deh-noon'-the-ah*
Statement	Declaración	*Deh-clah-rah-the-aun'*
Lawyer	Abogado	*Ah-bau-gah'-doh*
Theft	Robo	*Rau'-boh*
Mugging	Atraco	*Ah-trah'-coh*
Accident	Accidente	*Ac-the-dehn'-teh*
Passport	Pasaporte	*Pah-sah-paur'-teh*
Wallet	Cartera	*Car-teh'-rah*
Handbag	Bolso	*Baul'-soh*

Where is the nearest police station?	✎ ¿Dónde está la comisaría más próxima?
	💬 *Daun'-deh es-tah' lah cau-me-sah-ree'-ah mas prauc'-se-mah?*

I have come to report a ...	✎ Vengo a poner una denuncia
	💬 *Vehn'-goh ah pau-ner' oo'-nah deh-noon'-the-ah*

| My ... has been stolen | Me han robado el/la ... |
| | *Meh ahn rau-bah'-doh el/lah ...* |

| I have been assaulted | Me han golpeado |
| | *Meh ahn gaul-peh-ah'-doh* |

| My ... has disappeared from my room | Mi ... ha desaparecido de la habitación |
| | *Mee ... ah deh-sah-pah-reh-thee'-doh deh lah ah-be-tah-the-aun'* |

| I have lost my passport | Se me ha perdido el pasaporte |
| | *Seh meh ah per-dee'-doh el pah-sah-paur'-teh* |

| I have had a car accident | He tenido un accidente de coche |
| | *Eh teh-nee'-doh oon ac-the-dehn'-teh deh cau'-cheh* |

| I don't understand. Can I have an interpreter? | No entiendo. ¿Puedo venir un intérprete? |
| | *Noh en-te-ehn'-doh. Poo-eh'-doh veh-neer' oon in-ter'-preh-teh?* |

| Can I call my embassy (consulate)? | ¿Puedo llamar a mi embajada (consulado)? |
| | *Poo-eh'-doh lyah-mar' ah mee em-bah-hah'-dah (caun-soo-lah'-doh)?* |

| How should I fill out the report? | ¿Cómo debo cumplimentar la denuncia? |
| | *Cau'-moh deh'-boh coom-ple-men-tar' lah deh-noon'-the-ah?* |

TRAVEL DICTIONARY

ENGLISH-SPANISH

alcohol. alcohol. *al-cau-aul'*

all. todo. *tau'-doh*

allow. permitir. *per-me-teer'*

almost. casi. *cah'-se*

alone. solo. *sau'-loh*

along. por. *paur*

already. ya. *yah*

also. también. *tam-be-en'*

although. aunque. *ah'-oon-keh*

always. siempre. *se-ehm'-preh*

ambulance. ambulancia.
   am-boo-lahn'-the-ah

among. entre. *ehn'-treh*

amount. suma. *soo'-mah*

and. y. *ee*

another. otro. *au'-troh*

answer. respuesta. *res-poo-es'-tah*

any. algún. *al-goon'*

apartment. apartamento.
   ah-par-tah-mehn'-toh

apple. manzana. *man-thah'-nah*

appointment. cita. *thee'-tah*

arm. brazo. *brah'-thoh*

around. alrededor. *al-reh-deh-daur'*

arrive. llegar. *lyeh-gar'*

arrival. llegada. *lyeh-gah'-dah*

as. como, cuando.
   cau'-moh, coo-ahn'-doh

ask. preguntar. *preh-goon-tar'*

at. en, a. *en, ah*

attention. atención. *ah-ten-the-aun'*

August. agosto. *ah-gaus'-toh*

aunt. tía. *tee'-ah*

autumn. otoño. *au-tau'-nyoh*

avenue. avenida. *ah-veh-nee'-dah*

back. espalda, atrás.
   es-pahl'-dah, ah-tras'

bad. malo. *mah'-loh*

banana. plátano. *plah'-tah-noh*

bank. banco. *bahn'-coh*

bar. bar. *bar*

bath. baño. *bah'-nyoh*

bathroom. cuarto de baño.
   coo-ar'-toh deh bah'-nyoh

battery. pila, batería.
   pee'-lah, bah-teh-ree'-ah

be. ser. *ser*

beach. playa. *plah'-yah*

beautiful. bonito. *bau-nee'-toh*

because. porque. *paur'-keh*

bed. cama. *cah'-mah*

bedroom. dormitorio. *daur-me-tau'-re-oh*

beer. cerveza. *ther-veh'-thah*

before. antes. *ahn'-teh*

begin. empezar. *em-peh-thar'*

behind. detrás. *deh-tras'*

believe. creer. *creh-er'*

belt. cinturón. *thin-too-raun'*

beside. junto a. *hoon'-toh ah*

best, better. mejor. *meh-huur'*

between. entre. *ehn'-treh*

bicycle. bicicleta. *be-the-cleh'-tah*

big. grande. *grahn'-deh*

bill. cuenta. *coo-ehn'-tah*

bird. pájaro. *pah'-hah-roh*

biscuit. galleta. *gah-lyeh'-tah*

bitter. amargo. *ah-mar'-goh*

black. negro. *neh'-groh*

blanket. manta. *mahn'-tah*

blond. rubio. *roo'-be-oh*

blood. sangre. *sahn'-greh*

blue. azul. *ah-thool'*

body. cuerpo. *coo-er'-poh*

bone. hueso. *oo-eh'-soh*

book. libro. *lee'-broh*

boot. bota. *bau'-tah*

both. ambos. *ahm'-bohs*

bother. molestar. *mau-les-tar'*

bottle. botella. *bau-teh'-lyah*

box. caja. *cah'-hah*

boy. chico. *chee'-coh*

brake. freno. *freh'-noh*

bread. pan. *pahn*

breakdown. avería. *ah-veh-ree'-ah*

breakfast. desayuno. *deh-sah-yoo'-noh*

bridge. puente. *poo-ehn'-teh*

bring. traer. *trah-er'*

broken. roto. *rau'-toh*

brother. hermano. *er-mah'-noh*

brown. marrón. *mar-raun'*

brush. cepillo. *theh-pee'-lyoh*

building. edificio. *eh-de-fee'-the-oh*

bull. toro. *tau'-roh*

business. negocio. *neh-gau'-the-oh*

but. pero. *peh'-roh*

butcher's. carnicería. *car-ne-theh-ree'-ah*

butter. mantequilla. *man-teh-kee'-lyah*

buy. comprar. *caum'-prar'*

by. por, de. *paur, deh*

cabin. camarote. *cah-mah-rau'-teh*

cake. pastel, tarta. *pas-tehl', tar'-tah*

call. llamar, llamada. *lyah-mar', lyah-mah'-dah*

camera. cámara. *cah'-mah-rah*

can. poder, lata. *pau-der', lah'-tah*

cancel. cancelar. *can-theh-lar'*

car. coche. *cau'-cheh*

card. tarjeta, carta. *tar-heh'-tah, car'-tah*

carrot. zanahoria. *thah-nah-au'-re-ah*

carry. llevar. *lyeh-var'*

cash. cobrar, caja. *cau-brar', cah'-hah*

castle. castillo. *cas-tee'-lyoh*

cat. gato. *gah'-toh*

cathedral. catedral. *cah-teh-drahl'*

caution. cuidado. *coo-e-dah'-doh*

centre. centro. *thehn'-troh*

century. siglo. *see'-gloh*

chair. silla. *see'-lyah*

change. cambiar, cambio. *cam-be-ar', cahm'-be-oh*

cheap. barato. *bah-rah'-toh*

cheese. queso. *keh'-soh*

chemist's. farmacia. *far-mah'-the-ah*

cheque. cheque. *cheh'-keh*

cherry. cereza. *theh-reh'-thah*

child. niño. *nee'-nyoh*

chocolate. chocolate. *chau-cau-lah'-teh*

chop. chuleta. *choo-leh'-tah*

church. iglesia. *e-gleh'-se-ah*

cigar. puro. *poo'-roh*

cigarette. cigarrillo. *the-gar-ree'-lyoh*

cinema. cine. *thee'-neh*

city. ciudad. *the-oo-dad'*

class. clase. *clah'-seh*

clean. limpio. *leem'-pe-oh*

clear. claro. *clah'-roh*

climate. clima. *klee'-mah*

clinic. clínica. *klee'-ne-cah*

close. cerrar, cerca. *ther-rar', thehr'-cah*

closed. cerrado. *ther-rah'-doh*

clothes. ropa. *rau'-pah*

cloud. nube. *noo'-beh*

coach. autocar. *ah-oo-tau-car'*

coast. costa. *caus'-tah*

coat. abrigo. *ah-bree'-goh*

coin. moneda. *mau-neh'-dah*

cold. frío. *free'-oh*

colour. color. *cau-laur'*

comb. peinarse, peine. *peh-e-nar'-seh, peh'-e-neh*

come. venir. *veh-neer'*

concert. concierto. *caun-the-er'-toh*

constipation. estreñimiento. *es-treh-nye-me-en'-toh*

conversation. conversación. *caun-ver-sah-the-aun'*

cook. cocinar. *cau-the-nar'*

cool. fresco. *fres'-coh*

copy. copia. *cau'-pe-ah*

corn. maíz. *mah-eth'*

corner. esquina. *es-kee'-nah*

cost. costar. *caus-tar'*

cotton. algodón. *al-gau-daun'*

cough. tos. *taus*

counter. mostrador. *maus-trah-daur'*

country. país. *pah-ees'*

court. patio, pista. *pah'-te-oh, pees'-tah*

cousin. primo. *pree'-moh*

cow. vaca. *vah'-cah*

cream. nata. *nah'-tah*

credit. crédito. *creh'-de-toh*

cross. cruzar. *croo-thar'*

cup. taza. *tah'-thah*

custom. costumbre. *caus-toom'-breh*

customs. aduana. *ah-doo-ah'-nah*

cut. corte, cortar. *caur'-teh, caur-tar'*

daily. diario. *de-ah'-re-oh*

damage. daño. *dah'-nyoh*

danger. peligro. *peh-lee'-groh*

dark. oscuro. *aus-coo'-roh*

date. fecha. *feh'-chah*

daughter. hija. *ee'-hah*

day. día. *dee'-ah*

dead. muerto. *moo-er'-toh*

December. diciembre. *de-the-ehm'-breh*

deck. cubierta. *coo-be-er'-tah*

declare. declarar. *deh-clah-rar'*

delay. retraso. *reh-trah'-soh*

dentist. dentista. *den-tees'-tah*

departure. salida. *sah-lee'-dah*

dessert. postre. *paus'-treh*

dictionary. diccionario. *dic-the-au-nah'-re-oh*

die. morir. *mau-reer'*

difficult. difícil. *de-fee'-theel*

dinner. comida, cena. *cau-mee'-dah, theh'-nah*

direct. directo. *de-rec'-toh*

dirty. sucio. *soo'-the-oh*

discount. descuento. *des-coo-ehn'-toh*

dish. plato. *plah'-toh*

district. barrio. *bar'-re-oh*

disturb. molestar. *mau-les-tar'*

do. hacer. *ah-thehr'*

doctor. médico. *meh'-de-coh*

dog. perro. *per'-roh*

door. puerta. *poo-er'-tah*

double. doble. *dau'-bleh*

down. abajo. *ah-bah'-hoh*

dress. vestirse, vestido. *ves-teer'-seh, ves-tee'-doh*

drink. beber, bebida. *beh-ber', beh-bee'-dah*

drive. conducir. *caun-doo-theer'*

dry. seco. *seh'-coh*

duck. pato. *pah'-toh*

during. durante. *doo-rahn'-teh*

each. cada. *cah'-dah*

ear. oído, oreja. *au-ee'-doh, au-reh'-hah*

early. temprano. *tem-prah'-noh*

earth. tierra. *te-er'-rah*

east. este. *es'-teh*

easy. fácil. *fah'-theel*

eat. comer. *cau-mer'*

egg. huevo. *oo-eh'-voh*

eight. ocho. *au'-choh*

elbow. codo. *cau'-doh*

elder, eldest. mayor. *mah-yaur'*

eleven. once. *aun'-theh*

embassy. embajada. *em-bah-hah'-dah*

empty. vacío. *vah-thee'-oh*

end. fin, final. *feen, fe-nahl'*

engine. motor. *mau-taur'*

enough. bastante. *bas-tahn'-teh*

entry (entrance). entrada. *en-trah'-dah*

envelope. sobre. *sau'-breh*

evening. tarde, noche.
 tar'-deh, nau'-cheh

every. cada. *cah'-dah*

example. ejemplo. *eh-hehm'-ploh*

excess. exceso. *ex-theh'-soh*

exchange. cambio. *cahm'-be-oh*

excuse. disculpar, perdonar.
 dis-cool-par', per-dau-nar'

exhibition. exposición.
 ex-pau-se-the-aun'

exit. salida. *sah-lee'-dah*

eye. ojo. *au'-hoh*

face. cara. *cah'-rah*

factory. fábrica. *fah'-bre-cah*

family. familia. *fah-mee'-le-ah*

far. lejos. *leh'-hohs*

fare. tarifa. *tah-ree'-fah*

fashion. moda. *mau'-dah*

fast. rápido. *rah'-pe-doh*

father. padre. *pah'-dreh*

February. febrero. *feh-breh'-roh*

ferry. transbordador.
 trans-baur-dah-daur'

few. pocos. *pau'-cohs*

field. campo. *cahm'-poh*

fill. llenar, empastar.
 lyeh-nar', em-pas-tar'

filling station. gasolinera.
 gah-sau-le-neh'-rah

film. película. *peh-lee'-coo-lah*

filter. filtro. *feel'-troh*

find. encontrar. *en-caun-trar'*

fine. bonito, multa.
 bau-nee'-toh, mool'-tah

finger. dedo. *deh'-doh*

finish. terminar. *ter-me-nar'*

fire. fuego. *foo-eh'-goh*

first. primero. *pre-meh'-roh*

fish. pescado. *pes-cah'-doh*

five. cinco. *theen'-coh*

flavour. sabor. *sah-baur'*

flight. vuelo. *voo-eh'-loh*

floor. piso, planta. *pee'-soh, plahn'-tah*

flower. flor. *flaur*

follow. seguir. *seh-gheer'*

food. comida. *cau-mee'-dah*

foot. pie. *pe-eh'*

for. para. *pah'-rah*

forbidden. prohibido. *prau-e-bee'-doh*

foreign(er). extranjero. *ex-tran-heh'-roh*

fork. tenedor. *teh-neh-daur'*

forget. olvidar. *aul-ve-dar'*

fountain. fuente. *foo-ehn'-teh*

free. libre, gratis. *lee'-breh, grah'-tis*

Friday. viernes. *ve-er'-nehs*

fried. frito. *free'-toh*

friend. amigo. *ah-mee'-goh*

from. de, desde. *deh, des'-deh*

fruit. fruta. *froo'-tah*

full. lleno. *lyeh'-noh*

furniture. mueble. *moo-eh'-bleh*

gallon. galón. *gah-laun'* (4,5 l.)

game. juego. *hoo-eh'-goh*

garage. garaje. *gah-rah'-heh*

garden. jardín. *har-deen'*

garlic. ajo. *ah'-hoh*

gate. puerta. *poo-er'-tah*

gentleman. caballero. *cah-bah-lyeh'-roh*

gift. regalo. *reh-gah'-loh*

girl. chica. *chee'-cah*

give. dar. *dar*

glad. contento. *caun-tehn'-toh*

glass. vaso, cristal. *vah'-soh, cris-tahl'*

glasses. gafas. *gah'-fahs*

glove. guante. *goo-ahn'-teh*

go. ir. *eer*

go out. salir. *sah-leer'*

gold. oro. *au'-roh*

good. bueno. *boo-eh'-noh*

good bye. adiós. *ah-de-aus'*

grape. uva. *oo'-vah*

great. gran, grande. *grahn, grahn'-deh*

green. verde. *ver'-deh*

greeting. saludo. *sah-loo'-doh*

grey. gris. *grees*

group. grupo. *groo'-poh*

guide. guía. *ghee'-ah*

habit. costumbre. *caus-toom'-breh*

hair. pelo. *peh'-loh*

half. mitad, medio. *me-tad', meh'-de-oh*

ham. jamón. *hah-maun'*

hand. mano. *mah'-noh*

handbag. bolso. *baul'-soh*

happen. pasar, ocurrir.
pah-sar', au-coor-reer'

happy. feliz. *feh-leeth'*

harbour. puerto. *poo-er'-toh*

hat. sombrero. *saum-breh'-roh*

have. tener, haber. *teh-ner', ah-ber'*

have lunch. almorzar. *al-maur-thar'*

he. él. *el*

head. cabeza. *cah-beh'-thah*

health. salud. *sah-lood'*

hear. oír. *au-eer'*

heart. corazón. *cau-rah-thaun'*

heavy. pesado. *peh-sah'-doh*

help. ayudar, socorro.
ah-yoo-dar', sau-caur'-roh

her. su, la, le. *soo, lah, leh*

high. alto. *ahl'-toh*

him. lo, le. *lau, leh*

hire. alquilar. *al-ke-lar'*

his. su. *soo*

holidays. vacaciones.
vah-cah-the-au'-nes

holy. santo. *sahn'-toh*

home. casa, hogar. *cah'-sah, au-gar'*

honey. miel. *me-ehl'*

hope. esperar. *es-peh-rar'*

horse. caballo. *cah-bah'-lyoh*

hospital. hospital. *aus-pe-tahl'*

hot. caliente. *cah-le-ehn'-teh*

hotel. hotel. *au-tehl'*

hour. hora. *au'-rah*

house. casa. *cah'-sah*

how. cómo. *cau'-moh*

hunger. hambre. *ahm'-breh*

hurry. prisa. *pree'-sah*

hurt. herida, daño.
eh-ree'-dah, dah'-nyoh

husband. marido. *mah-ree'-doh*

ice. hielo. *e-eh'-loh*

ice cream. helado. *eh-lah'-doh*

if. si. *see*

ill. enfermo. *en-fer'-moh*

in. en, dentro de. *en, dehn'-troh deh*

inch. pulgada. *pool-gah'-dah* (2,5 cm.)

included. incluido. *in-cloo-ee'-doh*

indigestion. indigestión.
in-de-hes-te-oun'

influenza. gripe. *gree'-peh*

injured. herido. *eh-ree'-doh*

interest. interés. *in-teh-res'*

interesting. interesante.
in-teh-reh-sahn'-teh

interpreter. intérprete.
in-ter'-preh-teh

into. en. *en*

introduce. presentar. *preh-sen-tar'*

invite. invitar. *in-vee-tar'*

iron. hierro, plancha.
e-er'-roh, plahn'-chah

island. isla. *ees'-lah*

it. lo. *lau*

jacket. chaqueta. *chah-keh'-tah*

jam. mermelada. *mer-meh-lah'-dah*

January. enero. *eh-neh'-roh*

jeans. vaqueros. *vah-keh'-rohs*

jewel. joya. *hau'-yah*

jeweller's. joyería. *hau-yeh-ree'-ah*

journey. viaje. *ve-ah'-heh*

juice. zumo. *thoo'-moh*

July. julio. *hoo'-le-oh*

June. junio. *hoo'-ne-oh*

key. llave. *lyah'-veh*

kidney. riñón. *re-nyaun'*

kind. amable, tipo.
ah-mah'-bleh, tee'-poh

kitchen. cocina. *cau-thee'-nah*

knee. rodilla. *rau-dee'-lyah*

knife. cuchillo. *coo-chee'-lyoh*

know. saber, conocer.
sah-ber', cau-nau-thehr'

lady. señora. *seh-nyau'-rah*

lake. lago. *lah'-goh*

lamp. lámpara. *lahm'-pah-rah*

land. tierra, aterrizar.
te-er'-rah, ah-ter-re-thar'

language. lengua, idioma.
lehn'-goo-ah, e-de-au'-mah

large. grande. *grahn'-deh*

last. último. *ool'-te-moh*

last night. anoche. *ah-nau'-cheh*

late. tarde. *tar'-deh*

later. luego. *loo eh'-goh*

laundry. lavandería. *lah-van-deh-ree'-ah*

learn. aprender. *ah-pren-der'*

leather. piel. *pe-ehl'*

leave. salir, irse. *sah-leer', eer'-seh*

left. izquierdo. *eth-ke-er'-doh*

leg. pierna. *pe-er'-nah*

leisure. tiempo libre.
te-ehm'-poh lee'-breh

lemon. limón. *lee-maun'*

less. menos. *meh'-nohs*

letter. carta, letra. *car'-tah, leh'-trah*

lettuce. lechuga. *leh-choo'-gah*

library. biblioteca. *be-ble-au-teh'-cah*

life. vida. *vee'-dah*

lift. ascensor. *as-thehn-saur'*

light. luz, ligero. *looth, le-heh'-roh*

lighter. encendedor.
en-thehn-deh-daur'

like. gustar, como. *goos-tar', cau'-moh*

line. línea. *lee'-neh-ah*

lip. labio. *lah'-be-oh*

listen. escuchar. *es-coo-char'*

little. pequeño, poco.
peh-keh'-nyoh, pau'-coh

live. vivir. *ve-veer'*

liver. hígado. *ee'-gah-doh*

lodging. alojamiento.
ah-lau-hah-me-en'-toh

long. largo. *lar'-goh*

look. mirar. *me-rar'*

look for. buscar. *boos-car'*

lorry. camión. *cah-me-aun'*

lost. perdido. *per-dee'-doh*

loud. alto. *ahl'-toh*

low. bajo. *bah'-hoh*

luck. suerte. *soo-er'-teh*

luggage. equipaje. *eh-ke-pah'-heh*

lunch. almuerzo. *al-moo-er'-thoh*

lung. pulmón. *pool-maun'*

luxury. lujo. *loo'-hoh*

machine. máquina. *mah'-ke-nah*

madam. señora. *seh-nyau'-rah*

made. hecho. *eh'-choh*

magazine. revista. *reh-vees'-tah*

mail. correo. *caur-reh'-oh*

main. principal. *prin-the-pahl'*

make. hacer. *ah-thehr'*

man. hombre. *aum'-breh*

many. muchos. *moo'-chohs*

map. mapa. *mah'-pah*

March. marzo. *mar'-thoh*

market. mercado. *mer-cah'-doh*

marmalade. mermelada de naranja.
mer-meh-lah'-dah deh nah-rahn'-hah

married. casado. *cah-sah'-doh*

match. cerilla. *theh-ree'-lyah*

mattress. colchón. *caul-chaun'*

May. mayo. *mah'-yoh*

me. mí. *mee*

meal. comida. *cau-mee'-dah*

meaning. significado. *sig-ne-fe-cah'-doh*

means. medios. *meh'-de-ohs*

measure. medida. *meh-dee'-dah*

meat. carne. *car'-neh*

mechanic. mecánico. *meh-cah'-ne-coh*

medicine. medicina. *meh-de-thee'-nah*

melon. melón. *meh-laun'*

message. recado, mensaje.
reh-cah'-doh, men-sah'-heh

mild. suave. *soo-ah'-veh*

mile. milla. *mee'-lyah* (1,6 km)

milk. leche. *leh'-cheh*

million. millón. *me-lyaun'*

minute. minuto. *me-noo'-toh*

mirror. espejo. *es-peh'-hoh*

miss. señorita. *seh-nyau-ree'-tah*

mistake. error. *er-raur'*

mister. señor. *seh-nhyaur'*

missis. señora. *seh-nyau'-rah*

mixed. mixto. *mix'-toh*

modern. modern. *mau-der'-noh*

moment. momento. *mau-mehn'-toh*

Monday. lunes. *loo'-nehs*

money. dinero. *de-neh'-roh*

month. mes. *mehs*

monument. monumento.
mau-noo-mehn'-toh

moon. luna. *loo'-nah*

more. más. *mahs*

morning. mañana. *mah-nyah'-nah*

mother. madre. *mah'-dreh*

motorway. autopista.
ah-oo-toh-pees'-tah

mountain. montaña.
maun-tah'-nyah

mouth. boca. *bau'-cah*

much. mucho. *moo'-choh*

museum. museo. *moo-seh'-oh*

music. música. *moo'-se-cah*

must. deber. *deh-ber'*

my. mi, mis. *mee, mees*

name. nombre. *naum'-breh*

narrow. estrecho. *es-treh'-choh*

near. cerca. *thehr'-cah*

necessary. necesario.
neh-theh-sah'-re-oh

neck. cuello. *coo-eh'-lyoh*

need. necesitar. *neh-theh-se-tar'*

neighbour. vecino. *veh-thee'-noh*

neither. ni. *nee*

nephew. sobrino. *sau-bree'-noh*

never. nunca. *noon'-cah*

new. nuevo. *noo-eh'-voh*

news. noticia. *nau-tee'-the-ah*

newsagent's. quiosco. *ke-aus'-coh*

newspaper. periódico.
peh-re-au'-de-coh

next. próximo, siguiente.
  prauc'-se-moh, se-ghe-ehn'-teh
nice. agradable. *ah-grah-dah'-bleh*
niece. sobrina. *sau-bree'-nah*
night. noche. *nau'-cheh*
nine. nueve. *noo-eh'-veh*
no. no, ningún. *noh, nin-goon'*
nobody. nadie. *nah'-de-eh*
noise. ruido. *roo-ee'-doh*
none. ninguno. *nin-goo'-noh*
noon. mediodía. *meh-de-au-dee'-ah*
nor. ni. *nee*
north. norte. *naur'-teh*
nose. nariz. *nah-reeth'*
not. no. *noh*
nothing. nada. *nah'-dah*
notice. aviso. *ah-vee'-soh*
noun. nombre. *naum'-breh*
November. noviembre.
  nau-ve-ehm'-breh
now. ahora. *ah-au'-rah*
number. número. *noo'-meh-roh*
nurse. enfermera. *en-fer-meh'-rah*

o'clock. en punto. *en poon'-toh*
October. octubre. *auc-too'-breh*
of. de. *deh*
offer. ofrecer, oferta.
  au-freh-thehr', au-fer'-tah
office. oficina. *au-fe-thee'-nah*
often. a menudo. *ah meh-noo'-doh*

oil. aceite. *ah-theh'-e-teh*
old. viejo. *ve-eh'-hoh*
olive. aceituna. *ah-the-e-too'-nah*
on. en, sobre. *en, sau' breh*
once. una vez. *oo'-nah vehth'*
one. uno. *oo'-noh*
onion. cebolla. *theh-bau'-lyah*
only. sólo, solamente.
  sau'-loh, sau-lah-mehn'-teh
open. abierto. *ah-be-er'-toh*
opposite. enfrente. *en-frehn'-teh*
optician's. óptica. *aup'-te-cah*
or. o. *oh*
orange. naranja. *nah-ran'-hah*
orchestra. orquesta. *aur-kes'-tah*
order. orden, pedir. *aur'-den, peh-deer'*
other. otro. *au'-troh*
ounce. onza. *aun'-thah* (28 gr)
our. nuestro. *noo-es'-troh*
out. fuera. *foo-eh'-rah*
out of order. averiado.
  ah-veh-re-ah'-doh
over. encima. *en-thee'-mah*
owe. deber. *de-neh'-roh*
owner. dueño. *doo-eh'-nyoh*

package. paquete, bulto.
  pah-keh'-teh, bool'-toh
pain. dolor. *dau-laur'*
painting. pintura. *pin-too'-rah*
pair. par. *par*

palace. palacio. *pah-lah'-the-oh*

paper. papel. *pah-pehl'*

parcel. paquete. *pah-keh'-teh*

pardon. perdón. *per-daun'*

parents. padres. *pah'-drehs*

park. parque, aparcar.
par'-keh, ah-par-car'

parking. aparcamiento.
ah-par-cah-me-ehn'-toh

part. parte. *par'-teh*

party. partido, fiesta.
par-tee'-doh, fe-es'-tah

passenger. pasajero. *pah-sah-heh'-roh*

passport. pasaporte. *pah-sah-paur'-teh*

pavement. acera. *ah-theh'-rah*

pay. pagar. *pah-gar'*

peach. melocotón. *meh-lau-cau-taun'*

pear. pera. *peh'-rah*

pedestrian. peatón. *peh-ah-taun'*

pen. pluma. *ploo'-mah*

pencil. lápiz. *lah'-peth*

people. gente. *hehn'-teh*

pepper. pimienta. *pe-me-ehn'-tah*

perhaps. tal vez. *tahl veth'*

permission. permiso. *per-mee'-soh*

person. persona. *per-sau'-nah*

petrol. gasolina. *gah-sau-lee'-nah*

photograph. foto. *fau'-toh*

pick up. recoger. *reh-cau-her'*

picture. cuadro. *coo-ah'-droh*

pie. pastel, tarta. *pas-tehl', tar'-tah*

piece. pieza, trozo.
pe-eh'-thah, trau'-thoh

pill. pastilla. *pas-tee'-lyah*

pillow. almohada. *al-mau-ah'-dah*

pineapple. piña. *pee'-nyah*

pink. rosa. *rau'-sah*

pint. pinta. *peen'-tah* (0,5 l.)

pity. lástima. *las'-te-mah*

place. lugar, sitio. *loo-gar', see'-te-oh*

plan. plano. *plah'-noh*

plane. avión. *ah-ve-aun'*

plant. planta. *plahn'-tah*

platform. andén. *an-dehn'*

play. jugar, tocar. *hoo-gar', tau-car'*

please. por favor. *paur fah-vaur'*

plum. ciruela. *the-roo-eh'-lah*

pocket. bolsillo. *baul-see'-lyoh*

point. punto. *poon'-toh*

police. policía. *pau-le-thee'-ah*

police station. comisaría.
cau-me-sah-ree'-ah

poor. pobre. *pau'-breh*

pork. cerdo. *ther'-doh*

port. puerto. *poo-er'-toh*

post office. Correos. *caur-reh'-ohs*

potato. patata. *pah-tah'-tah*

pound. libra. *lee'-brah*

prefer. preferir. *preh-feh-reer'*

prepare. preparar. *preh-pah-rar'*

prescription. receta.
reh-theh'-tah

present. presente, regalo.
preh-sehn´-teh, reh-gah´-loh

pretty. guapo, bonito.
goo-ah´-poh, bau-nee´-toh

price. precio. *preh´-the-oh*

problem. problema. *prau-bleh´-mah*

promenade. paseo. *pah-seh´-oh*

pudding. pudín. *poo-deen´*

pull. tirar. *te-rar´*

pullover. jersey. *her-seh´-y*

puncture. pinchazo. *pin-chah´-thoh*

push. empujar. *em-poo-har´*

put. poner. *pau-ner´*

put in. meter. *meh-ter´*

quarter. cuarto. *coo-ar´-toh*

quay. muelle. *moo-eh´-lyeh*

question. pregunta. *preh-goon´-tah*

queue. cola. *cau´-lah*

quick. rápido. *rah´-pi-doh*

quiet. tranquilo, callado.
tran-kee´-loh, cah-lyah´-doh

rain. llover, lluvia.
lyau-ver´, lyoo´-ve-ah

raw. crudo. *croo´-doh*

reach. llegar. *lyeh-gar´*

read. leer. *leh-er´*

ready. listo. *lees´-toh*

reason. causa, razón.
cah´-oo-sah, rah-thaun´

receive. recibir. *reh-the-beer´*

recommend. recomendar.
reh-cau-men-dar´

record. disco. *dees´-coh*

red. rojo. *rau´-hoh*

reduction. reducción.
reh-dooc-the-aun

regards. saludo. *sah-loo´-doh*

relatives. parientes.
pah-re-eln´-tehs

remember. recordar. *reh-caur-dar´*

rent. alquilar. *al-ke-lar´*

repair. reparar. *reh-pah-rar´*

repeat. repetir. *reh-peh-teer´*

reply. respuesta. *res-poo-es´-tah*

restaurant. restaurante.
res-tah-oo-rahn´-teh

return. volver, vuelta.
vaul-ver´, voo-el´-tah

rice. arroz. *ar-rauth´*

rich. rico. *ree´-coh*

right. derecho, correcto.
deh-reh´-choh, caur-rec´-toh

river. río. *ree´-oh*

road. calle, carretera. *car-reh-teh´-rah*

roast. asado. *ah-sah´-doh*

room. habitación. *ah-be-tah-the-aun´*

round. redondo. *reh-daun´-doh*

row. fila. *fee´-lah*

safe. seguro. *seh-goo´-roh*

sail. navegar. *nah-veh-gar'*

salad. ensalada. *en-sah-lah'dah*

sale. venta. *vehn'-tah*

sales. rebajas. *reh-bah'-hahs*

salt. sal. *sahl*

same. mismo. *mees'-moh*

sand. arena. *ah-reh'-nah*

Saturday. sábado. *sah'-bah-doh*

sauce. salsa. *sahl'-sah*

sausage. salchicha. *sahl-chee'-chah*

say. decir. *deh-theer'*

school. escuela. *es-coo-eh'-lah*

scissors. tijeras. *te-heh'-rahs*

sea. mar. *mar*

season. estación. *es-tah-the-aun'*

seat. asiento. *ah-se-ehn'-toh*

second. segundo. *seh-goon'-doh*

see. ver. *ver*

sell. vender. *vehn-der'*

send. mandar, enviar.
man-dar', en-ve-ar'

September. Septiembre.
Sep-te-em'-breh

serve. servir. *ser-veer'*

seven. siete. *se-eh'-teh*

several. varios. *vah'-re-ohs*

she. ella. *eh'-lyah*

sheet. sábana. *sah'-bah-nah*

ship. barco. *bar'-coh*

shirt. camisa. *cah-mee'-sah*

shoe. zapato. *thah-pah'-toh*

shop. tienda. *te-ehn'-dah*

short. corto. *caur'-toh*

shower. ducha. *doo'-chah*

sick. enfermo. *en-fer'-moh*

side. lado. *lah'-doh*

sign. signo, firmar. *seeg'-noh, fir-mar'*

silence. silencio. *se-lehn'-the-oh*

silk. seda. *seh'-dah*

silver. plata. *plah'-tah*

since. desde. *dehs'-deh*

sing. cantar. *cahn-tar'*

single. individual, soltero.
in-de-ve-doo-ahl', saul-teh'-roh

sir. señor. *seh-nyaur'*

sister. hermana. *er-mah'-nah*

sit down. sentarse. *sehn-tar'-seh*

six. seis. *seh'-es*

size. tamaño, talla.
tah-mah'-nyoh, tah'-lyah

skin. piel. *pe-ehl'*

sleep. dormir. *daur-meer'*

slow. lento. *lehn'-toh*

small. pequeño. *peh-keh'-nyoh*

smoke. fumar. *foo-mar'*

snow. nieve. *ne-eh'-veh*

so. así. *ah-see'*

soap. jabón. *hah-baun'*

soft. suave. *soo-ah'-veh*

some. algunos. *ahl-goo'-nohs*

son. hijo. *ee'-hoh*

soon. pronto. *praun'-toh*

sorry. perdón, lo siento.
per-daun', lau se-ehn'-toh

sort. tipo, clase. *tee'-poh, clah'-seh*

soup. sopa. *sau'-pah*

south. sur. *soor*

souvenir. recuerdo. *reh-coo-er'-doh*

Spanish. español. *es-pah-nyaul'*

speak. hablar. *ah-blar'*

speed. velocidad. *veh-lau-the-dad'*

spoon. cuchara. *coo-chah'-rah*

sport. deporte. *deh-paur'-teh*

spring. primavera. *pre-mah-veh'-rah*

square. plaza, cuadrado.
plah'-thah, coo-ah-drah'-doh

stairs. escalera. *es-cah-leh'-rah*

stamp. sello. *seh'-lyoh*

start. empezar. *em-peh-thar'*

station. estación. *es-tah-the-aun'*

steak. filete. *fe-leh'-teh*

steal. robar. *rau-bar'*

stewardess. azafata. *ah-thah-fah'-tah*

stomach. estómago. *es-tau'-mah-goh*

stop. parar, parada.
pah-rar', pah-rah'-dah

strawberry. fresa. *freh'-sah*

street. calle. *cah'-lyeh*

strike. huelga. *oo-ehl'-gah*

strong. fuerte. *foo-er'-teh*

suburb. barrio. *bar'-re-oh*

such. tal. *tahl*

sugar. azúcar. *ah-thoo'-car*

suit. traje. *trah'-heh*

suitcase. maleta. *mah-leh'-tah*

summer. verano. *veh-rah'-noh*

sun. sol. *sohl'*

Sunday. domingo. *dau-meen'-goh*

sure. seguro. *seh-goo'-roh*

surgery. consulta. *caun-sool'-tah*

surname. apellido. *ah-peh-lyee'-doh*

sweet. dulce. *dool'-theh*

swim. nadar. *nah-dar'*

swimming pool. piscina. *pes-thee'-nah*

table. mesa. *meh'-sah*

tablet. pastilla. *pas-tee'-lyah*

take. tomar, coger. *tau-mar', cau-her*

talk. hablar. *ah-blar'*

tall. alto. *ahl'-toh*

tax. impuesto. *im-poo-es'-toh*

tea. té. *teh*

telephone. teléfono. *teh-leh'-fau-noh*

tell. decir, contar. *deh-theer', caun-tar'*

temperature. temperatura.
tem-peh-rah-too'-rah

ten. diez. *de-eth'*

tent. tienda de campaña.
te-ehn'-dah deh cahm-pah'-nyah

terrace. terraza. *ter-rah'-thah*

than. que. *keh*

thanks. gracias. *grah'-the-ahs*

that. que. *keh*

the. el, la, los, las. *ehl, lah, lohs, lahs*

theatre. teatro. *teh-ah'-troh*

their. su, sus. *soo, soos*

then. entonces. *en-taun'-thehs*

there. allí. *ah-lyee'*

these. estos, estas. *es'-tohs, es'-tahs*

think. pensar. *pehn-sar'*

third. tercero. *ter-theh'-roh*

this. este, esta. *es'-teh, es'-tah*

thousand. mil. *meel*

three. tres. *tres*

throat. garganta. *gar-gahn'-tah*

Thursday. jueves. *hoo-eh'-vehs*

ticket. billete, entrada.
be-lyeh'-teh, en-trah'-dah

tie. corbata. *caur-bah'-tah*

time. tiempo. *te-ehm'-poh*

tip. propina. *prau-pee'-nah*

to. a, para. *ah, pah'-rah*

toast. tostada. *taus-tah'-dah*

tobacco. tabaco. *tah-bah'-coh*

together. juntos. *hoon'-tohs*

toilets. servicios. *ser-vee'-the-ohs*

toll. peaje. *peh-ah'-heh*

tomato. tomate. *tau-mah'-teh*

tomorrow. mañana. *mah-nyah'-nah*

tonight. esta noche. *es'-tah nau'-cheh*

too, too much/many. demasiado.
deh-mah-se-ah'-doh

tool. herramienta. *er-rah-me-ehn'-tah*

tooth. diente. *de-ehn'-teh*

towel. toalla. *tau-ah'-lyah*

tower. torre. *taur'-reh*

town. ciudad. *the-oo-dad'*

toy. juguete. *hoo-gheh'-teh*

traffic-lights. semáforo.
seh-mah'-fau-roh

train. tren. *trehn*

tram. tranvía. *trahn-vee'-ah*

translate. traducir. *trah-doo-theer'*

travel. viajar, viaje.
ve-ah-har', ve-ah'-heh

tree. árbol. *ar'-baul*

trip. viaje. *ve-ah'-heh*

trouble. molestar. *mau-les-tar'*

trousers. pantalones.
pahn-tah-lau'-nehs

truth. verdad. *ver-dad'*

try. tratar, probar. *trah-tar', prau-bar'*

Tuesday. martes. *mar'-tehs*

twelve. doce. *dau'-theh*

twenty. veinte. *veh'-in-teh*

twice. dos veces. *daus veh'-thehs*

two. dos. *daus*

tyre. neumático. *neh-oo-mah'-te-coh*

ugly. feo. *feh'-oh*

umbrella. paraguas. *pah-rah'-goo-ahs*

uncle. tío. *tee'-oh*

under. debajo. *deh-bah'-hoh*

underground. metro. *meh'-troh*

understand. comprender, entender.
caum-prehn-der', en-tehn-der'

until. hasta. *as'-tah*

up. arriba. *ar-ree'-bah*

urgent. urgente. *oor-hehn'-teh*

use. usar, uso. *oo-sar', oo'-soh*

vacant. libre. *lee'-breh*

value. valor. *vah-laur'*

van. furgoneta. *foor-gau-neh'-tah*

vegetables. verdura. *ver-doo'-rah*

very. muy. *moo'-y*

view. vista. *vees'-tah*

village. pueblo. *poo-eh'-bloh*

vinegar. vinagre. *ve-nah'-greh*

visa. visado. *ve-sah'-doh*

visit. visitar, visita. *vi-si-tar', vi-see'-tah*

voice. voz. *vauth*

wait. esperar. *es-peh-rar'*

walk. andar. *ahn-dar'*

wall. pared. *pah-red'*

wallet. cartera. *car-teh'-rah*

warm. cálido. *cah'-le-doh*

wash. lavar. *lah-var'*

watch. reloj. *reh-lau'*

water. agua. *ah'-goo-ah*

way. camino, manera.
  cah-mee'-noh, mah-neh'-rah

we. nosotros. *nau-sau'-trohs*

wear. llevar. *lyeh-var'*

weather. tiempo. *te-ehm'-poh*

Wednesday. miércoles. *me-er'-cau-lehs*

week. semana. *seh-mah'-nah*

weight. peso. *peh'-soh*

welcome. bienvenido.
  be-ehn-veh-nee'-doh

well. bien. *be-ehn'*

West. oeste. *au-es'-teh*

what. qué, lo que. *keh', lau keh*

wheel. rueda. *roo-eh'-dah*

when. cuándo. *coo-ahn'-doh*

where. dónde. *daun'-deh*

which. cuál. *coo-ahl'*

white. blanco. *blahn'-coh*

who. quién. *ke-ehn'*

whole. todo. *tau'-doh*

why. por qué. *paur keh'*

wide. ancho. *ahn'-choh*

wife. esposa, mujer.
  es-pau'-sah, moo-her'

wind. viento. *ve-ehn'-toh*

window. ventana. *vehn-tah'-nah*

wine. vino. *vee'-noh*

winter. invierno. *in-ve-er'-noh*

wish. desear. *deh-seh-ar'*

with. con. *caun*

without. sin. *seen*

woman. mujer. *moo-her'*

wool. lana. *lah'-nah*

word. palabra. *pah-lah'-brah*

work. trabajar, trabajo.
  trah-bah-har', trah-bah'-hoh

world. mundo. *moon'-doh*

worse. peor. *peh-aur′*

write. escribir. *es-cre-beer′*

yacht. yate. *yah′-teh*

yard. yarda. *yar′-dah* (1,6 km)

year. año. *ah′-nyoh*

yellow. amarillo. *ah-mah-ree′-lyoh*

yes. sí. *see*

yesterday. ayer. *ah-yer′*

you. tú, vosotros.
 too, vau-sau′-trohs

young. joven. *jau′-vehn*

your. tu, vuestro. *too, voo-es′-troh*

zero. cero. *theh′-roh*

zoo. zoo. *thau′-oh*

SPANISH-ENGLISH

a. *ah.* to, at

abajo. *ah-bah´-hoh.* down, downstairs

abierto. *ah-be-er´-toh.* open

abrigo. *ah-bree´-goh.* coat

abril. *ah-breel´.* April

abrir. *ah-breer´.* open

acabar. *ah-cah-bar´.* to finish

accidente. *ak-the-dehn´-teh.* accidente

aceite. *ah-theh´-e-teh.* oil

aceituna. *ah-theh-e-too´-nah.* olive

acelerador. *ah-theh-leh-rah-daur´.* accelerator

aceptar. *ah-thep-tar´.* to accept

acera. *ah-theh´-rah.* pavement

aconsejar. *ah-caun-seh-har´.* to advise

acuerdo (de...). *deh ah-coo-er´-doh.* all right

adelante. *ah-deh-lahn´-teh.* ahead

además. *ah-deh-mas´.* besides

adiós. *ah-de-aus´.* good bye

aduana. *ah-doo-ah´-nah.* customs

afeitarse. *ah-feh-e-tar´-seh.* to shave

agencia. *ah-hehn´-the-ah.* agency

agosto. *ah-gaus´-toh.* August

agradable. *ah-grah-dah´-bleh.* nice

agrio. *ah´-gre-oh.* sour

agua. *ah´-goo-ah.* water

ahí. *ah-ee´.* there

ahora. *ah-au´-rah.* now

ahorro. *ah-aur´-roh.* saving

aire. *ah´-e-reh.* air

ajo. *ah´-hoh.* garlic

alcohol. *al-cau-aul´.* alcohol

algo. *ahl´-goh.* something

algodón. *ahl-gau-daun´.* cotton

almohada. *al-mau-ah´-dah.* pillow

almorzar. *al-maur-thar´.* to have lunch

alojamiento. *ah-lau-hah-me-ehn´-toh.* lodging

alquilar. *al-kee-lar´.* to rent, to hire

alrededor. *al-reh-deh-daur´.* around

alto. *ahl´-toh.* tall, high

allí. *ah-lyee´.* there

amable. *ah-mah´-bleh.* kind

amarillo. *ah-mah-ree´-lyoh.* yellow

amargo. *ah-mar´-goh.* bitter

ambos. *ahm´-bohs.* both

ambulancia. *am-boo-lahn´-the-ah.* ambulance

amigo. *ah-mee´-goh.* friend

ancho. *ahn´-choh.* wide

andar. *an-dar´.* to walk

andén. *an-dehn´.* platform

anoche. *ah-nau´-cheh.* last night

anuncio. *ah-noon'-the-oh.* advertisement

antes. *ahn'-tehs.* before

año. *ah'-nyoh.* year

apellido. *ah-peh-lyee'-doh.* surname

aparcar. *ah-par-car'.* to park

aparcamiento. *ah-par-cah-me-ehn'-toh.* parking

apartamento. *ah-par-tah-mehn'-toh.* apartment

aprender. *ah-pren-der'.* to learn

aquel. *ah-kehl'.* that

aquí. *ah-kee'.* here

árbol. *ar'-baul.* tree

arena. *ah-reh'-nah.* sand

arriba. *ar-ree'-bah.* up, upstairs

arroz. *ar-rauth'.* rice

artesanía. *ar-teh-sah-nee'-ah.* handicraft

asado. *ah-sah'-doh.* roast

ascensor. *as-then-saur'.* lift

así. *ah-see'.* so

asunto. *ah-soon'-toh.* affair

asiento. *ah-se-ehn'-toh.* seat

atención. *ah-ten-the-aun'.* attention

aterrizar. *ah-ter-re-thar'.* to land

atrás. *ah-tras'.* back

atún. *ah-toon'.* tuna

aunque. *ah'-oon-keh.* although

autobús. *ah-oo-tau-boos'.* bus

autocar. *ah-oo-tau-car'.* coach

autopista. *ah-oo-toh-pees'-tah.* motorway

avería. *ah-veh-ree'-ah.* breakdown

averiado. *ah-veh-re-ah'-doh.* out of order

avión. *ah-ve-aun'.* plane

aviso. *ah-vee'-soh.* notice

ayer. *ah-yer'.* yesterday

ayudar. *ah-yoo-dar'.* to help

ayuntamiento. *ah-yoon-tah-me-ehn'-toh.* town hall

azafata. *ah-thah-fah'-tah.* stewardess

azúcar. *ah-thoo'-car.* sugar

azul. *ah-thool'.* blue

bacalao. *bah-cah-lah'-oh.* cod

bajo. *bah'-hoh.* low, short

banco. *bahn'-coh.* bank

bañarse. *bah-nyar'-seh.* to bathe

baño. *bah'-nyoh.* bath

bar. *bahr.* bar

barato. *bah-rah'-toh.* cheap

barba. *bar'-bah.* beard

barco. *bar'-coh.* ship

barrio. *bar'-re-oh.* district

bastante. *bas-tahn'-teh.* enough

beber. *beh-ber'.* to drink

bebida. *beh-bee'-dah.* drink

biblioteca. *be-ble-au-teh'-cah.* library

bicicleta. *be-the-cleh'-tah.* bicycle

bien. *be-en'.* well

bienvenido. *be-en-veh-nee´-doh.* welcome

blanco. *blahn´-coh.* white

boca. *bau´-cah.* mouth

bolso. *baul´-soh.* handbag

bolsillo. *baul-see´-lyoh.* pocket

bonito. *bau-nee´-toh.* pretty

bota. *bau´-tah.* boot

botella. *bau-teh´-lyah.* bottle

brazo. *brah´-thoh.* arm

bueno. *boo-eh´-noh.* good

buscar. *boos-car´.* to look for

buzón. *boo-thaun´.* pillar box

caballero. *cah-bah-lyeh´-roh.* gentleman

caballo. *cah-bah´-lyoh.* horse

cabello. *cah-beh´-lyoh.* hair

cabeza. *cah-beh´-thah.* head

cada. *cah´-dah.* each, every

café. *cah-feh´.* coffee

cafetería. *cah-feh-teh-ree´-ah.* coffee house

caja. *cah´-hah.* box, cash

caliente. *cah-le-ehn´-teh.* hot

calmante. *cal-mahn´-teh.* sedative

calor. *cah-laur´.* heat

calle. *cah´-lyeh.* street

cama. *cah´-mah.* bed

cámara. *cah´-mah-rah.* camera

camarero. *cah-mah-reh´-roh.* waiter

camarote. *cah-mah-rau´-teh.* cabin

cambiar. *cam-be-ar´.* to change

cambio. *cahm´-be-oh.* change, exchange

camino. *cah-mee´-noh.* way

camión. *cah-me-aun´.* lorry

camisa. *cah-mee´-sah.* shirt

campo. *cahm´-poh.* country, field

cara. *cah´-rah.* face

carne. *car´-neh.* meat

carnicería. *car-ne-theh-ree´-ah.* butcher's

caro. *cah´-roh.* expensive

carretera. *car-reh-teh´-rah.* road

carta. *car´-tah.* letter

cartera. *car-the´-rah.* wallet

casado. *cah-sah´-doh.* married

casi. *cah´-see.* almost, nearly

castillo. *cas-tee´-lyoh.* castle

catedral. *cah-teh-drahl´.* cathedral

catorce. *cah-taur´-theh.* fourteen

cebolla. *theh-bau´-lyah.* onion

cena. *theh´-nah.* dinner, supper

cenicero. *theh-ne-theh´-roh.* ashtray

centro. *thehn´-troh.* centre

cepillo. *theh-pee´-lyoh.* brush

cerca. *ther´-cah.* near

cerdo. *ther´-doh.* pork, pig

cereza. *theh-reh´-thah.* cherry

cerilla. *theh-ree´-lyah.* match

cero. *theh´-roh.* zero

cerrado. *ther-rah'-doh.* closed
cerrar. *ther-rar'.* to close
cerveza. *ther-veh'-thah.* beer
chaleco. *chah-leh'-coh.* vest
chaqueta. *chah-keh'-tah.* jacket
cheque. *cheh'-keh.* cheque
chico/a. *chee'-coh/ah.* boy, girl
chocolate. *chau-cau-lah'-teh.* chocolate
chuleta. *choo-leh'-tah.* chop
cielo. *the-eh'-loh.* sky
cien. *the-ehn'.* one hundred
cigarrillo. *the-gar-ree'-lyoh.* cigarette
cinco. *theen'-coh.* five
cine. *thee'-neh.* cinema
ciruela. *the-roo-eh'-lah.* plum
cita. *thee'-tah.* apointment
ciudad. *the-oo-dad'.* town, city
claro. *clah'-roh.* clear, light
clase. *clah'-seh.* class, kind, sort
cliente. *cle-ehn'-teh.* customer, client
clima. *clee'-mah.* climate
cobrar. *cau-brar'.* to cash
cocido. *cau-thee'-doh.* boiled
coche. *cau'-cheh.* car
cocina. *cau-thee'-nah.* kitchen
codo. *cau'-doh.* elbow
coger. *cau-her'.* to catch, to take
col. *caul.* cabbage
cola. *cau'-lah.* queue, tail
colchón. *caul-chaun'.* mattress
coliflor. *cau-li-flaur'.* cauliflower

comedor. *cau-meh-daur'.* dining room
comenzar. *cau-men-thar'.* to begin
comer. *cau-mer'.* to eat
comida. *cau-mee'-dah.* meal, food
comisaría. *cau-me-sah-ree'-ah.*
  police station
como. *cau'-moh.* how, as, like
comprar. *caum-prar'.* to buy
comprender. *caum-pren-der'.*
  to understand
con. *caun.* with
conducir. *caun-doo-theer'.* to drive
conmigo. *caun-mee'-goh.* with me
conocer. *cau-nau-thehr'.* to know
consejo. *caun-seh'-hoh.* advice
consigna. *caun-seeg'-nah.*
  left-luggage office
consulado. *caun-soo-lah'-doh.*
  consulate
consulta. *caun-sool'-tah.* surgery
contar. *caun-tar'.* to tell, to count
contento. *caun-tehn'-toh.* glad
contestar. *caun-tes-tar'.* to answer
contigo. *caun-tee'-goh.* with you
contra. *caun'-trah.* against
copa. *cau'-pah.* (wine) glass
corazón. *cau-rah-thaun'.* heart
corbata. *caur-bah'-tah.* tie
cordero. *caur-deh'-roh.* lamb
correo. *caur-reh'-oh.* mail
Correos. *caur-reh'-ohs.* post office

cortar. *caur-tar'.* to cut

corto. *caur'-toh.* short

cosa. *cau'-sah.* thing

cosecha. *cau-seh'-chah.* vintage

costa. *caus'-tah.* coast

costumbre. *caus-toom'-breh.* custom, habit

cotización. *cau-te-thah-the-aun'.* rate

crema. *creh'-mah.* cream

cristal. *crees-tahl'.* glass, lens

cruce. *croo'-theh.* croosroads

crudo. *croo'-doh.* raw

cuadro. *coo-ah'-droh.* picture

cuál. *coo-ahl'.* which

cualquiera. *coo-ahl-ke-eh'-rah.* any

cuando. *coo-ahn'-doh.* when

cuánto. *coo-ahn'-toh.* how much/many

cuarenta. *coo-ah-rehn'-tah.* forty

cuarto. *coo-ar'-toh.* quarter, fourth, room

cuatro. *coo-ah'-troh.* four

cubierta. *coo-be-er'-tah.* cover, deck

cuchara. *coo-chah'-rah.* spoon

cuchillo. *coo-chee'-lyoh.* knife

cuello. *coo-eh'-lyoh.* neck, collar

cuenta. *coo-ehn'-tah.* bill, account

cuerpo. *coo-er'-poh.* body

cuidado. *coo-e-dah'-doh.* care, attention

curva. *coor'-vah.* bend, curve

daño. *dah'-nyoh.* damage

dar. *dar.* to give

de. *deh.* of, from

debajo. *deh-bah'-hoh.* down, downstairs

deber. *deh-ber'.* must, to owe

decir. *deh-theer'.* to say, to tell

dedo. *deh'-doh.* finger, toe

dejar. *deh-har'.* to leave, to let

delante. *deh-lahn'-teh.* in front

demasiado. *deh-mah-se-ah'-doh.* too, too much/many

dentro. *dehn'-troh.* inside

deporte. *deh-paur'-teh.* sport

derecho. *deh-reh'-choh.* right, straight

desayuno. *deh-sah-yoo'-noh.* breakfast

descuento. *des-coo-ehn'-toh.* discount

desde. *des'-deh.* from

desear. *deh-seh-ar'.* to want

despacio. *des-pah'-the-oh.* slowly

después. *des-poo-es'.* after

detrás. *deh-tras'.* behind

día. *dee'-ah.* day

diario. *de-ah'-re-oh.* daily

dibujo. *deh-boo'-hoh.* drawing

diccionario. *dek-the-au-nah'-re-oh.* dictionary

diciembre. *de-the-ehm'-breh.* December

diente. *de-ehn'-teh.* tooth

diez. *de-eth'.* ten

difícil. *de-fee'-thil.* difficult

dinero. *de-neh'-roh.* money

dirección. *de-rek-the-aun'.*
direction, address

directo. *de-rek'-toh.* direct

disco. *dees'-coh.* record

diversión. *de-ver-se-aun'.*
entertainment

divisa. *de-vee'-sah.* foreign currency

doble. *dau'-bleh.* double

doce. *dau'-theh.* twelve

docena. *dau-theh'-nah.* dozen

dolor. *dau-laur'.* pain, ache

domingo. *dau-meen'-goh.* Sunday

donde. *daun'-deh.* where

dormir. *daur-meer'.* to sleep

dormitorio. *daur-me-tau'-re-oh.*
bedroom

dos. *daus.* two

ducha. *doo'-chah.* shower

dueño. *doo-eh'-nyoh.* owner

dulce. *dool'-theh.* sweet

durante. *doo-rahn'-teh.* during

durar. *doo-rar'.* to last

duro. *doo'-roh.* hard

edad. *eh-dad'.* age

edificio. *eh-de-fee'-the-oh.* building

ejemplo. *eh-hehm'-ploh.* example

él. *el.* he

ella. *eh'-lyah.* she

embajada. *em-bah-hah'-dah.* embassy

embrague. *em-brah'-gheh.* clutch

empezar. *em-peh-thar'.*
to begin, to start

empleado. *em-pleh-ah'-doh.* employee

empresa. *em-preh'-sah.* enterprise

empujar. *em-poo-har'.* to push

en. *ehn.* in, on

encendedor. *en-then-deh-daur'.* lighter

encima. *en-thee'-mah.* above, over

encontrar. *en-caun-trar'.*
to find, to meet

enero. *eh-neh'-roh.* January

enfermedad. *en-fer-meh-dad'.*
illness, disease

enfermera. *en-fer-meh'-rah.* nurse

enfermo. *en-fer'-moh.* ill, sick

enfrente. *en-frehn'-teh.* opposite

ensalada. *en-sah-lah'-dah.* salad

enseñar. *en-seh-nyar'.*
to teach, to show

entender. *en-ten-der'.* to understand

entero. *en-teh'-roh.* whole

entonces. *en-taun'-thes.* then

entrada. *en-trah'-dah.* entrance, ticket

entre. *ehn'-treh.* between, among

enviar. *en-ve-ar'.* to send

equipaje. *eh-ke-pah'-heh.* luggage

error. *er-raur'.* mistake

escalera. *es-cah-leh'-rah.* stairs

escribir. *es-cre-beer'.* to write

escuchar. *es-coo-char'.* to listen

escuela. *es-coo-eh'-lah.* school

ese. *eh'-seh.* that

espalda. *es-pahl'-dah.* back

español. *es-pah-nyaul'.* Spanish

espectáculo. *es-pek-tah'-coo-loh.* spectacle

espejo. *es-peh'-hoh.* mirror

esperar. *es-peh-rar'.* to wait, to hope

espuma. *es-poo'-mah.* foam

esquina. *es-kee'-nah.* corner

estación. *es-tah-the-aun'.* station, season

estanco. *es-tahn'-coh.* tobacconist's

estar. *es-tar'.* to be

este. *es'-teh.* this, East

estómago. *es-tau'-mah-goh.* stomach

estrecho. *es-treh'-choh.* narrow, tight

estrella. *es-treh'-lyah.* star

estreñimiento. *es-treh-nye-me-ehn'-toh.* constipation

etiqueta. *eh-te-keh'-tah.* label

exposición. *ex-pau-se-the-aun'.* exhibition

extranjero. *ex-tran-heh'-roh.* foreign(er)

fábrica. *fah'-bre-cah.* factory

fácil. *fah'-thil.* easy

factura. *fak-too'-rah.* invoice

falda. *fahl'-dah.* skirt

familia. *fah-mee'-le-ah.* family

farmacia. *far-mah'-the-ah.* chemist's

favor (por...). *paur fah-vaur'.* please

febrero. *feh-breh'-roh.* February

fecha. *feh'-chah.* date

feliz. *feh-leeth'.* happy

feo. *feh'-oh.* ugly

fiebre. *fe-eh'-breh.* fever

fiesta. *fe-es'-tah.* party

fila. *fee'-lah.* row, line

filete. *fe-leh'-teh.* steak

filtro. *feel'-troh.* filter

fin(al). *feen, fe-nahl'.* end

firmar. *fer-mar'.* to sign

flan. *flahn.* caramel custard

flor. *flaur.* flower

folleto. *fau-lyeh'-toh.* brochure

foto. *fau'-toh.* photograph

freno. *freh'-noh.* brake

fresa. *freh'-sah.* strawberry

fresco. *fres'-coh.* cool, fresh

frigorífico. *fri-gau-ree'-fe-coh.* fridge

frío. *free'-oh.* cold

frito. *free'-toh.* fried

frontera. *fraun-teh'-rah.* frontier

fruta. *froo'-tah.* fruit

fuego. *foo-eh'-goh.* fire

fuente. *foo-ehn'-teh.* fountain

fuera. *foo-eh'-rah.* out, outside

fuerte. *foo-er'-teh.* strong

fumar. *foo-mar'.* to smoke

función. *foon-the-aun'.* show

furgoneta. *foor-gau-neh´-tah.* van

gafas. *gah´-fahs.* glasses

galleta. *gah-lyeh´-tah.* biscuit

gallina. *gah-lyee´-nah.* hen

garaje. *gah-rah´heh.* garage

garganta. *gar-gahn´-tah.* throat

gasolina. *gah-sau-lee´-nah.* petrol

gasolinera. *gah-sau-le-neh´-rah.*
filling station

gato. *gah´-toh.* cat, jack

gazpacho. *gath-pah´-choh.*
vegetable cold soup

gente. *hehn´-teh.* people

ginebra. *ge-neh´-brah.* gin

gracias. *grah´-the-ahs.* thanks

grado. *grah´-doh.* degree

gran(de). *grahn´(deh).*
big, great, large

gratis. *grah´-tees.* free

grifo. *gree´-foh.* tap

gripe. *gree´-peh.* influenza

gris. *grees.* grey

guante. *goo-ahn´-teh.* glove

guía. *ghee´-ah.* guide

guisante. *ghe-sahn´-teh.* pea

gustar. *goos-tar´.* to like

haber. *ah-ber´.* to have

habitación. *ah-be-tah-the-aun´.* room

hablar. *ah-blar´.* to speak, to talk

hacer. *ah-thehr´.* to do, to make

hacia. *ah´-the-ah.* towards

hambre. *ahm´-breh.* hunger

harina. *ah-ree´-nah.* flour

hasta. *as´-tah.* until

hecho. *eh´-choh.* fact, done, made

helado. *eh-lah´-doh.* ice-cream

herido. *eh-ree´-doh.* injured, wounded

hermano/a. *er-mah´-noh/ah.*
brother, sister

herramlenta. *er-rah-me-ehn´-tah.* tool

hervido. *er-vee´-doh.* boiled

hielo. *e-eh´-loh.* ice

hierro. *e-er´-roh.* iron

hígado. *ee´-gah-doh.* liver

hijo/a. *ee´-hoh/-ah.* son, daughter

hola. *au´-lah.* hello

hombre. *aum´-breh.* man

hora. *au´-rah.* hora

hospital. *aus-pe-tahl´.* hospital

hotel. *au-tehl´.* hotel

hoy. *au´-y.* today

huelga. *oo-ehl´-gah.* strike

hueso. *oo-eh´-soh.* bone

huevo. *oo-eh´-voh.* egg

idioma. *e-de-au´-mah.* language

iglesia. *e-gleh´-se-ah.* church

igual. *e-goo-ahl´.* same, equal

impermeable. *im-per-meh-ah´-bleh.*
raincoat

impuesto. *im-poo-es´-toh.* tax

incluido. *in-cloo-ee'-doh.* included

indigestión. *in-de-hes-te-aun'.* indigestion

individual. *in-de-ve-doo-ahl'.* single

información. *in-faur-mah-the-aun'.* information

inglés. *in-glés.* English

invitar. *in-ve-tar'.* to try

intentar. *in-ten-tar'.* to try

interés. *in-teh-res'.* interest

interesante. *in-teh-reh-sahn'-teh.* interesting

intérprete. *in-ter'-preh-teh.* interpreter

invierno. *in-ve-er'-noh.* winter

ir. *eer.* to go

isla. *ees'-lah.* island

izquierdo. *ith-ke-er'-doh.* left

jabón. *hah-baun'.* soap

jamón. *hah-maun'.* ham

jarabe. *hah-rah'-beh.* syrup

jardín. *har-deen'.* garden

jefe. *heh'-feh.* chief, boss

jersey. *her-seh'-y.* pullover

joven. *hau'-vehn.* young

joya. *hau'-yah.* jewel

joyería. *hau-yeh-ree'-ah.* jeweller's

juego. *hoo-eh'-goh.* play, game

jueves. *hoo-eh'-vehs.* Thursday

jugar. *hoo-gar'.* to play

juguete. *hoo-gheh'-teh.* toy

julio. *hoo'-le-oh.* July

junio. *hoo'-ne-oh.* June

juntos. *hoon'-tohs.* together

kilo(gramo). *kee'-loh (grah-moh).* kilogramme

kilómetro. *kee-lau'-meh-troh.* kilometre

la. *lah.* the (fem.), her

labio. *lah'-be-oh.* lip

lado. *lah'-doh.* side

lago. *lah'-goh.* lake

lámpara. *lahm'-pah-rah.* lamp

lana. *lah'-nah.* wool

lápiz. *lah'-pith.* pencil

largo. *lar'-goh.* long

lástima. *las'-te-mah.* pity

lata. *lah'-tah.* tin, can

lavar. *lah-var'.* to wash

lavandería. *lah-van-deh-ree'-ah.* laundry

le. *leh.* him, her

leche. *leh'-cheh.* milk

lechuga. *leh-choo'-gah.* lettuce

leer. *leh-er'.* to read

lejos. *leh'-hohs.* far

lengua. *lehn'-goo-ah.* language, tongue

lento. *lehn'-toh.* slow

letra. *leh'-trah.* letter

ley. *leh'-y.* law

libre. *lee'-breh.* free, vacant

librería. *le-breh-ree'-ah.* bookshop

libro. *lee'-broh.* book

licor. *le-caur'.* liqueur

ligero. *le-heh'-roh.* light

limón. *le-maun'.* lemon

limpio. *leem'-pe-oh.* clean

línea. *lee'-neh-ah.* line

líquido. *lee'-ke-doh.* liquid, fluid

litera. *le-teh'-rah.* couchette

llamada. *lyah-mah'-dah.* call

llamar. *lyah-mar'.* to call, to phone

llave. *lyah'-veh.* key

lleno. *lyeh'-noh.* full

llegada. *lyeh-gah'-dah.* arrival

llegar. *lyeh-gar'.* to arrive

llevar. *lyeh-var'.* to carry, to wear

llover. *lyau-ver'.* to rain

lluvia. *lyoo'-ve-ah.* rain

lo. *lau.* it, him

lomo. *lau'-moh.* loin

luego. *loo-eh'-goh.* later

lugar. *loo-gar'.* place

lujo. *loo'-hoh.* luxury

luna. *loo'-nah.* moon

luz. *looth.* light

madera. *mah-deh'-rah.* wood

madre. *mah'-dreh.* mother

maíz. *mah-ith'.* corn

mal. *mahl.* bad, badly

maleta. *mah-leh'-tah.* suitcase

malo. *mah'-loh.* bad

mandar. *man-dar'.* to send

manera. *mah-neh'-rah.* way, manner

manga. *mahn'-gah.* sleeve

mano. *mah'-noh.* hand

manta. *mahn'-tah.* blanket

mantel. *man-tehl'.* tablecloth

mantequilla. *man-teh-kee'-lyah.* butter

manzana. *man-thah'-nah.* apple

mañana. *mah-nyah'-nah.* tomorrow, morning

mapa. *mah'-pah.* map

máquina. *mah'-ke-nah.* machine

mar. *mar.* sea

marca. *mar'-cah.* mark

mareo. *mah-reh'-oh.* seasickness

marido. *mah-ree'-doh.* husband

marisco. *mah-rees'-coh.* seafood

marrón. *mar-raun'.* brown

martes. *mar'-tehs.* Tuesday

marzo. *mar'-thoh.* March

más. *mas.* more

matrícula. *mah-tree'-coo-lah.* number-plate

mayo. *mah'-yoh.* May

mayor. *mah-yaur'.* bigger, older, larger

me. *meh.* me

mecánico. *meh-cah'-ne-coh.* mechanic

medianoche. *meh-de-ah-nau'-cheh.* midnight

medicina. *meh-de-thee'-nah.* medicine

médico. *meh'-de-coh.* doctor

medida. *meh-dee'-dah.* measure

medio. *meh'-de-oh.* half, middle

mediodía. *meh-de-oh-dee'-ah.* midday, noon

mejor. *meh-haur'.* better, best

melocotón. *meh-lau-cau-taun'.* peach

melón. *meh-laun'.* melon

menor. *meh-naur'.* smaller, younger

menos. *meh'-nohs.* less, least

mensaje. *men-sah'-heh.* message

menudo (a...). *ah meh-noo'-doh.* often

mercado. *mer-cah'-doh.* market

merluza. *mer-loo'-thah.* hake

mermelada. *mer-meh-lah'-dah.* jam

mes. *mes.* month

mesa. *meh'-sah.* table

metro. *meh'-troh.* metre, underground

mezcla. *meth'-clah.* mixture

mi. *mee.* my

mí. *mee'.* me

miel. *me-ehl'.* honey

mientras. *me-ehn'-trahs.* while

miércoles. *me-er'-cau-lehs.* Wednesday

mil. *meel.* thousand

milla. *mee'-lyah.* mile

millón. *me-lyaun'.* million

minuto. *me-noo'-toh.* minute

mío. *mee'-oh.* mine

mirar. *me-rar'.* to look

mismo. *mees'-moh.* same

mitad. *me-tad'.* half

mixto. *meex'-toh.* mixed

moda. *mau'-dah.* fashion

modo. *mau'-doh.* way

molestar. *mau-les-tar'.* to disturb

momento. *mau-mehn'-toh.* moment

moneda. *mau-neh'-dah.* coin, currency

montaña. *maun-tah'-nyah.* mountain

monumento. *mau-noo-mehn'-toh.* monument

moreno. *mau-reh'-noh.* dark-haired

morir. *mau-reer'.* to die

mostaza. *maus-tah'-thah.* mustard

mostrador. *maus-trah-daur'.* counter

motivo. *mau-tee'-voh.* reason

moto. *mau'-toh.* motorcycle

muchacho/a. *moo-chah'-choh/ah.* boy, girl

mucho. *moo'-choh.* much

mueble. *moo-eh'-bleh.* furniture

muelle. *moo-eh'-lyeh.* quay

muerto. *moo-er'-toh.* dead

mujer. *moo-her'.* woman, wife

multa. *mool'-tah.* fine

mundo. *moon'-doh.* world

museo. *moo-seh'-oh.* museum

música. *moo'-se-cah.* music

muy. *moo'-y.* very

nacer. *nah-ther'.* to be born

nacimiento. *nah-the-me-ehn'-toh.* birth

nada. *nah'-dah.* nothing

nadar. *nah-dar'.* to swim

nadie. *nah'-de-eh.* nobody

naranja. *nah-rahn'-hah.* orange

nariz. *nah-rith'.* nose

navegar. *nah-veh-gar'.* to sail

nata. *nah'-tah.* cream

naturalmente. *nah-too-rahl-mehn'-teh.* naturally

Navidad. *nah-ve-dad'.* Christmas

necesario. *neh-theh-sah'-re-oh.* necessary

necesitar. *neh-theh-se-tar'.* to need

negocio. *neh-gau'-the-oh.* business

negro. *neh'-groh.* black

neumático. *neh-oo-mah'-te-coh.* tyre

nevar. *neh-var'.* to snow

ni. *nee.* nor, neither

niebla. *ne-eh'-blah.* fog

nieve. *ne-eh'-veh.* snow

ningún/a. *nen-goon'/ah.* no, not any

niño/a. *nee'-noh/ah.* child

no. *noh.* no, not

noche. *nau'-cheh.* night

nombre. *naum'-breh.* name, noun

norte. *naur'-teh.* north

nos. *nohs.* us

nosotros. *nau-sau'-trohs.* we

noticia. *nau-tee'-the-ah.* news

noveno. *nau-veh'-noh.* ninth

noviembre. *nau-ve-ehm'-breh.* November

nube. *noo'-beh.* cloud

nuestro. *noo-es'-troh.* our, ours

nueve. *noo-eh'-veh.* nine

nuevo. *noo-eh'-voh.* new

número. *noo'-meh-roh.* number

nunca. *noon'-cah.* never

o. *oh.* or

objeto. *aub-heh'-toh.* object, purpose

obra. *au'-brah.* work, play

ocasión. *au-cah-se-aun'.* chance

ocho. *au'-choh.* eight

ocio. *au'-the-oh.* leisure

octavo. *auc-tah'-voh.* eighth

octubre. *auc-too'-breh.* October

ocupado. *au-coo-pah'-doh.* occupied

oeste. *au-es'-teh.* west

oferta. *au-fer'-tah.* offer

oficina. *au-fe-thee'-nah.* office

ofrecer. *au-freh-thehr'.* to offer

oído. *au-ee'-doh.* ear

oír. *au-eer'.* to hear

ojo. *au'-hoh.* eye

ola. *au'-lah.* wave

olor. *au-laur'.* smell

olvidar. *aul-ve-dar'.* to forget

once. *aun'-theh.* eleven

óptica. *aup'-te-cah.* optician's

orden. *aur'-den.* order

oreja. *au-reh'-hah.* ear

orilla. *au-ree'-lyah.* shore

oro. *au'-roh.* gold

orquesta. *aur-kes'-tah.* orchestra

os. *aus.* you

oscuro. *aus-coo'-roh.* dark

otoño. *au-tau'-nyoh.* autumn

otro. *au'-troh.* another, other

padre. *pah'-dreh.* father

padres. *pah'-drehs.* parents

pagar. *pah-gar'.* to pay

página. *pah'-he-nah.* page

país. *pah-ees'.* country

paisaje. *pah-e-sah'-heh.* landscape

pájaro. *pah'-hah-roh.* bird

palabra. *pah-lah'-brah.* word

palacio. *pah-lah'-the-oh.* palace

palmera. *pal-meh'-rah.* palmtree

pan. *pahn.* bread

panadería. *pah-nah-deh-ree'-ah.* baker's

pantalones. *pan-tah-lau'-nehs.* trousers

pañuelo. *pah-nyoo-eh'-loh.* handkerchief

papel. *pah-pehl'.* paper

paquete. *pah-keh'-teh.* parcel, package

par. *par.* pair

para. *pah'-rah.* to, in order to, for

parada. *pah-rah'-dah.* stop

paraguas. *pah-rah'-goo-ahs.* umbrella

parar. *pah-rar'.* to stop

pared. *pah-red'.* wall

pariente. *pah-re-ehn'-teh.* relative

parque. *par'-keh.* park

parte. *par'-teh.* part

partido. *par-tee'-doh.* party, match

pasado. *pah-sah'-doh.* last, past

pasajero. *pah-sah-heh'-roh.* passenger

pasaporte. *pah-sah-paur'-teh.* passport

paseo. *pah-seh'-oh.* walk, promenade

pasillo. *pah-see'-lyoh.* corridor

paso. *pah'-soh.* step, pass

pastel. *pas-tehl'.* pie, cake

pastilla. *pas-tee'-lyah.* tablet

patata. *pah-tah'-tah.* potato

patio. *pah'-te-oh.* courtyard

pato. *pah'-toh.* duck

pavo. *pah'-voh.* turkey

peaje. *peh-ah'-heh.* toll

peatón. *peh-ah-taun'.* pedestrian

pecho. *peh'-choh.* chest

pedazo. *peh-dah'-thoh.* piece, bit

pedir. *peh-deer'.* to ask for, to order

peinado. *peh-e-nah'-doh.* hair style

peine. *peh'-e-neh.* comb

película. *peh-lee'-coo-lah.* film

peligro. *peh-lee'-groh.* danger

peligroso. *peh-le-grau'-soh.* dangerous

pelo. *peh'-loh.* hair

peluquería. *peh-loo-keh-ree'-ah.* hairdresser's

pensar. *pen-sar'.* to think

pensión. *pen-se-aun'.* boarding-house

peor. *peh-aur'.* worse, worst

pepino. *peh-pee'-noh.* cucumber

pequeño. *peh-keh'-nyoh.* little, small

pera. *peh'-rah.* pear

perder. *per-der'.* to lose

perdón. *per-daun'.* pardon, sorry

periódico. *peh-re-au'-de-coh.* newspaper

permiso. *per-mee'-soh.* permission, licence

permitir. *per-me-teer'.* to permit, to allow

pero. *peh'-roh.* but

perro. *per'-roh.* dog

persona. *per-sau'-nah.* person

pesado. *peh-sah'-doh.* heavy

pescado. *pes-cah'-doh.* fish

peso. *peh'-soh.* weight

pie. *pe-eh'.* foot

piedra. *pe-eh'-drah.* stone

piel. *pe-ehl'.* skin, leather

pierna. *pe-er'-nah.* leg

pieza. *pe-eh'-thah.* part, piece

pila. *pee'-lah.* battery

pimienta. *pe-me-ehn'-tah.* pepper

pimiento. *pe-me-ehn'-toh.* (red, green) pepper

pinchazo. *pin-chah'-thoh.* puncture

pintura. *pin-too'-rah.* painting

piña. *pee'-nyah.* pineapple

piscina. *pes-thee'-nah.* swimming pool

piso. *pee'-soh.* flat, floor

planchar. *plan-char'.* to iron

plano. *plah' noh.* plan

planta. *plahn'-tah.* plant, floor

plata. *plah'-tah.* silver

plátano. *plah'-tah-noh.* banana

plato. *plah'-toh.* dish

playa. *plah'-yah.* beach

plaza. *plah'-thah.* square

plomo. *plau'-moh.* lead

pluma. *ploo'-mah.* pen

pobre. *pau'-breh.* poor

poco. *pau'-coh.* little, few

poder. *pau-der'.* can, may

policía. *pau-le-thee'-ah.* police, policeman

pollo. *pau'-lyoh.* chicken

poner. *pau-ner'.* to put

poquito. *pau-kee'-toh.* little

por. *paur.* by, for, because of

porque. *paur'-keh.* because

por *qué.* *paur keh'.* why

postal. *paus-tahl'.* postcard

postre. *paus'-treh.* dessert

precio. *preh'-the-oh.* price

pregunta. *preh-goon'-tah.* question

preguntar. *preh-goon-tar'.* to ask

prensa. *prehn'-sah.* press

preparar. *preh-pah-rar'.* to prepare

presentar. *preh-sen-tar'.* to introduce

primavera. *pre-mah-veh'-rah.* spring

primero. *pre-meh'-roh.* first

primo. *pree'-moh.* cousin

principal. *prin-the-pahl'.* main

principio. *prin-thee'-pe-oh.* beginning

prisa. *pree'-sah.* hurry

problema. *pro-bleh'-mah.* problem

prohibir. *prau-e-beer'.* to forbid

pronto. *praun'-toh.* soon

propiedad. *prau-pe-eh-dad'.* property

propina. *prau-pee'-nah.* tip

propio. *prau'-pe-oh.* own

propósito. *prau-pau'-se-toh.* purpose

próximo. *prauc'-se-moh.* next, close

pueblo. *poo-eh'-bloh.* village

puente. *poo-ehn'-teh.* bridge

puerta. *poo-er'-tah.* door

puerto. *poo-er'-toh.* port, harbour

pulmón. *pool-maun'.* lung

punto. *poon'-toh.* point

puro. *poo'-roh.* pure, cigar

que. *keh.* that, what

qué. *keh'.* what, which

quedarse. *keh-dar'-seh.* to stay

queja. *keh'-hah.* complaint

quemadura. *keh-mah-doo'-rah.* burn

querer. *keh-rer'.* to want, to love

queso. *keh'-soh.* cheese

quien. *ke-ehn'.* who

quince. *keen'-theh.* fifteen

quincena. *ken-theh'-nah.* fortnight

quinientos. *ke-ne-ehn'-tohs.*
five hundred

quinto. *keen'-toh.* fifth

quiosco. *ke-aus'-coh.* newsagent's

quizá(s). *ke-thah'(s).* perhaps

ramo. *rah'-moh.* bouquet

rápido. *rah'-pe-doh.* quick

rato. *rah'-toh.* while

razón. *rah-thaun'.* reason, cause

rebajas. *reh-bah'-hahs.* sales

recado. *reh-cah'-doh.* message

receta. *reh-theh'-tah.*
prescription, recipe

recibir. *reh-the-beer'.* to receive

reclamar. *reh-clah-mar'.* to claim

recoger. *reh-cau-her'.*
to collect, to pick up

recomendar. *reh-cau-men-dar'.*
to recommend, to advise

recordar. *reh-caur-dar'.* to remember

recto. *rek'-toh.* straight

recuerdo. *reh-coo-er'-doh.*
souvenir, regard

redondo. *reh-daun'-doh.* round

refresco. *reh-fres'-coh.* refreshment

regalo. *reh-gah'-loh.* present, gift

reloj. *reh-lau'.* watch

relleno. *reh-lyeh´-noh.* stuffed

remitente. *reh-me-tehn´-teh.* sender

reparar. *reh-pah-rar´.* to repair

repente (de...). *deh reh-pehn´-teh.* suddenly

repetir. *reh-peh-teer´.* to repeat

repuesto. *reh-poo-es´-toh.* spare

reservar. *reh-ser-var´.* to book, to reserve

resfriado. *res-fre-ah´-doh.* cold

respuesta. *res-poo-es´-tah.* answer

restaurante. *res-tah-oo-rahn´-teh.* restaurant

retraso. *reh-trah´-soh.* delay

revista. *reh-vees´-tah.* magazine

rico. *ree´-coh.* rich

riñón. *re-nyaun´.* kidney

río. *ree´-oh.* river

robar. *rau-bar´.* to steal

rodilla. *rau-dee´-lyah.* knee

rojo. *rau´-hoh.* red

ropa. *rau´-pah.* clothes

rosa. *rau´-sah.* rose, pink

roto. *rau´-toh.* broken

rubio. *roo´-be-oh.* blond

rueda. *roo-eh´-dah.* wheel

ruido. *roo-ee´-doh.* noise

ruta. *roo´-tah.* route

sábado. *sah´-bah-doh.* Saturday

sábana. *sah´-bah-nah.* sheet

saber. *sah-ber´.* to know

sabor. *sah-baur´.* taste, flavour

sal. *sahl.* salt

sala. *sah´-lah.* hall

salchicha. *sal-chee´-chah.* sausage

salida. *sah-lee´-dah.* departure, exit

salir. *sah-leer´.* to go out, to leave

salón. *sah-laun´.* living room

salsa. *sahl´-sah.* sauce

salud. *sah-lood´.* health, cheers

saludo. *sah-loo´-doh.* greeting

san(ta). *sahn(tah).* saint, holy

sangre. *sahn´-greh.* blood

se. *seh.* oneself, him/herself

seco. *seh´-coh.* dry

sed. *sed´.* thirst

seda. *seh´-dah.* silk

seguida (en...). *ehn seh-ghee´-dah.* at once

seguir. *seh-gheer´.* to follow, to go on

según. *seh-goon´.* according to

segundo. *seh-goon´-doh.* second

seguro. *seh-goo´-roh.* sure, safe

seis. *seh´-ees.* six

sello. *seh´-lyoh.* stamp

semana. *seh-mah´-nah.* week

semáforo. *seh-mah´-fau-roh.* traffic-lights

sencillo. *sen-thee´-lyoh.* simple

sentarse. *sen-tar´-seh.* to sit down

señal. *seh-nyahl´.* signal, sign

señor. *seh-nyaur'.* mister, sir

señora. *seh-nyau'-rah.* Mrs., madam

septiembre. *sep-te-ehm'-breh.* September

séptimo. *sep'-te-moh.* seventh

ser. *ser.* to be

servicio. *ser-vee'-the-oh.* service

servicios. *ser-vee'-the-ohs.* toilets

servilleta. *ser-ve-lyeh'-tah.* serviette

servir. *ser-veer'.* to serve

sexto. *sex'-toh.* sixth

si. *see.* if, whether

sí. *see'.* yes

siempre. *se-ehm'-preh.* always

sierra. *se-er'-rah.* mountain range

siesta. *se-es'-tah.* afternoon nap

siete. *se-eh'-teh.* seven

siglo. *see'-gloh.* century

significado. *seg-ne-fe-cah'-doh.* meaning

siguiente. *se-ghe-ehn'-teh.* next, following

silencio. *se-lehn'-the-oh.* silence

silla. *see'-lyah.* chair

simpático. *sem-pah'-te-coh.* nice

sin. *seen.* without

sitio. *see'-te-oh.* place, spot

sobre. *sau'-breh.* over, envelope

sobrino/a. *sau-bree'-noh/ah.* nephew, niece

socorro. *sau-caur'-roh.* help, aid

sol. *saul.* sun

solamente. *sau-lah-mehn'-teh.* only

solo. *sau'-loh.* alone, only

solomillo. *sau-lau-mee'-lyoh.* sirloin

soltero. *saul-teh'-roh.* single, unmarried

sombra. *saum'-brah.* shade

sombrero. *saum-breh'-roh.* hat

sonido. *sau-nee'-doh.* sound

sopa. *sau'-pah.* soup

su. *soo.* his, her, its, their

suave. *soo-ah'-veh.* soft, mild

subir. *soo-beer'.* to go up

suceso. *soo-theh'-soh.* event

sucio. *soo'-the-oh.* dirty

suelo. *soo-eh'-loh.* floor, ground

suerte. *soo-er'-teh.* luck

sur. *soor.* south

suyo. *soo'-yoh.* his, hers, theirs

tabaco. *tah-bah'-coh.* tobacco

tal. *tahl.* such

talla. *tah'-lyah.* size

taller. *tah-lyer'.* repair shop

tamaño. *tah-mah'-nyoh.* size

también. *tam-be-ehn'.* also, too

tampoco. *tam-pau'-coh.* not either

tan. *tahn.* so, as

tanto. *tahn'-toh.* so much/many

tapa. *tah-pah.* small dish of food

taquilla. *tah-kee'-lyah.* ticket office

tarde. *tar'-deh.* afternoon, late

tarifa. *tah-ree'-fah.* rate

tarjeta. *tar-heh'-tah.* card

tarta. *tar'-tah.* cake, tart

taza. *tah'-thah.* cup

te. *teh.* you, yourself

té. *teh'.* tea

teatro. *teh-ah'-troh.* theatre

techo. *teh'-choh.* ceilling

teléfono. *teh-leh'-fau-noh.* telephone

televisión. *teh-leh-ve-se-aun'.* T.V.

temperatura. *tem-peh-rah-too'-rah.* temperature

temprano. *tem-prah'-noh.* early

tenedor. *teh-neh-daur'.* fork

tener. *teh-nehr'.* to have, to possess

tercero. *ter-theh'-roh.* third

terminar. *ter-me-nar'.* to finish

ternera. *ter-neh'-rah.* veal

terraza. *ter-rah'-thah.* terrace

ti. *tee.* you

tiempo. *te-ehm-poh.* time, weather

tienda. *te-ehn'-dah.* shop, tent

tierra. *te-er'-rah.* earth, ground

tijeras. *te-heh'-rahs.* scissors

tinto. *teen'-toh.* red (wine)

tío/a. *tee'-oh/ah.* uncle, aunt

típico. *tee'-pi-coh.* typical

tirar. *tee-rar'.* to pull, to throw

toalla. *tau-ah'-lyah.* towel

tobillo. *tau-bee'-lyoh.* ankle

tocar. *tau-car'.* to touch, to play

todavía. *tau-dah-vee'-ah.* still, yet

todo. *tau'-doh.* all, the whole

tomar. *tau-mar'.* to take

tomate. *tau-mah'-teh.* tomato

torero. *tau-reh'-roh.* bullfighter

tormenta. *taur-mehn'-tah.* storm

toro. *tau'-roh.* bull

torre. *taur'-reh.* tower

tortilla. *taur-tee'-lyah.* omelet

tos. *taus.* cough

tostada. *taus-tah'-dah.* toast

trabajar. *trah-bah-har'.* to work

traducir. *trah-doo-theer'.* to translate

traer. *trah-er'.* to bring

traje. *trah'-heh.* dress, suit

tranquilo. *tran-kee'-loh.* quiet

tranvía. *tran-vee'-ah.* tram

tratar. *trah-tar'.* to try, to treat

travesía. *trah-veh-see'-ah.* crossing

trece. *treh'-theh.* thirteen

treinta. *treh'-in-tah.* thirty

tren. *trehn.* train

tres. *trehs.* three

trozo. *trau'-thoh.* piece, part

trueno. *troo-eh'-noh.* thunder

tu. *too.* your

tú. *too'.* you

turismo. *too-rees'-moh.* tourism

turista. *too-rees'-tah.* tourist

tuyo. *too'-yoh.* yours

último. _ool'-te-moh._ last, final

un/a. _oon/ah._ a, an

único. _oo'-ne-coh._ only (one)

uno. _oo'-noh._ one

urgente. _oor-hehn'-teh._ urgent

usar. _oo-sar'._ to use

usted. _oos-ted'._ you

útil. _oo'-til._ useful

uva. _oo'-vah._ grape

vaca. _vah'-cah._ cow

vacaciones. _vah-cah-the-au'-nehs._
  holidays

vacío. _vah-thee'-oh._ empty

vagón. _vah-gaun'._ coach

vale. _vah'-leh._ O.K.

valer. _vah-ler'._ to cost

valor. _vah-laur'._ value

valle. _vah'-lyeh._ valley

vaqueros. _vah-keh'-rohs._ jeans

varios. _vah'-re-ohs._ several

vaso. _vah'-soh._ glass

vecino. _veh-thee'-noh._ neighbour

veinte. _veh'-in-teh._ twenty

velocidad. _veh-lau-the-dad'._ speed

vender. _ven-der'._ to sell

venir. _veh-neer'._ to come

venta. _vehn'-tah._ sale

ventana. _ven-tah'-nah._ window

ventanilla. _ven-tah-nee'-lyah._
  ticket/car window

ver. _ver._ to see

verano. _veh-rah'-noh._ summer

verdad. _ver-dad'._ truth

verde. _ver'-deh._ green

verdura. _ver-doo'-rah._ vegetables

vestido. _ves-tee'-doh._ dress

vez. _veth._ time

vía. _vee'-ah._ track

viajar. _ve-ah-har'._ to travel

viaje. _ve-ah'-heh._ travel, trip

viajero. _ve-ah-heh'-roh._ traveller

vida. _vee'-dah._ life

viejo. _ve-eh'-hoh._ old

viento. _ve-ehn'-toh._ wind

viernes. _ve-er'-nehs._ Friday

vinagre. _ve-nah'-greh._ vinegar

vino. _vee'-noh._ wine

visado. _ve-sah'-doh._ visa

visita. _ve-see'-tah._ visit

visitar. _ve-se-tar'._ to visit

vista. _vees'-tah._ view, sight

viudo/a. _ve-oo'-doh/ah._ widow(er)

vivir. _ve-veer'._ to live

vivo. _vee'-voh._ alive

volante. _vau-lahn'-teh._ steering wheel

volver. _vaul-ver'._ to return

vosotros. _vau-sau'-trohs._ you

voz. _voth._ voice

vuelo. _voo-eh'-loh._ flight

vuelta. _voo-ehl'-tah._ return, turn

vuestro. _voo-es'-troh._ your, yours

y. *ee.* and

ya. *yah.* already

yate. *yah´-teh.* yacht

yo. *yoh.* I

zanahoria. *thah-nah-au´-re-ah.* carrot

zapatería. *thah-pah-teh-ree´-ah.* shoeshop

zapato. *thah-pah´-toh.* shoe

zoo. *thau´-oh.* zoo

zumo. *thoo´-moh.* juice

© Purificación Blanco Hernández
© Editorial Arguval
I.S.B.N.: 84-95948-90-7
Depósito Legal: MA-310-2007

Cover: Luis Ojeda
Design: Stella Ramos

Impreso en España - Printed in Spain
Imprime Top Printer Plus, S.L.L.